ALSO BY ROY WEPNER

The Postwarriors: Boomers Aging Badly (2007)

Untethered: Problem Solving Unshackled by Rhyme or Reason (2016)

HOW TERRIBLY STRANGE INDEED

Seventy Is More Than Just a Number

ROY WEPNER

authorHOUSE®

AuthorHouse™
1663 Liberty Drive
Bloomington, IN 47403
www.authorhouse.com
Phone: 833-262-8899

Published by AuthorHouse 06/09/2022

ISBN: 978-1-6655-6181-5 (sc)
ISBN: 978-1-6655-6180-8 (e)

Print information available on the last page.

This book is printed on acid-free paper.

CONTENTS

DEDICATION

For my beloved wife SHELLEY WEPNER, who turned 70 while I was writing this book. Shelley is the strongest, wisest, most caring and most energetic person I have ever known. She has done a yeoman's job of saving me from myself on countless occasions, especially since I turned 70. (Why she hasn't yet taken away my car keys will have to remain our secret.) If there is anyone who can successfully navigate her way through her 70s and reinvent an even better version of herself, it is Shelley.

And for my beloved brother STEPHEN WEPNER, who graduated out his 70s shortly before I began this book. Steve started babysitting me during the Truman administration, always preparing me for the slings and arrows of the next stage of life. To the extent I have avoided many pitfalls, I have Steve to thank. To the extent I have not, I take full credit.

CHAPTER 1

HELLO, STRANGER

It was never supposed to happen. Not sooner. Not later. Not now. Not ever.

It was pretty much unimaginable.

We were the post-World War II baby boom generation. We were young. If we had anything to say about it—and we had something to say about pretty much everything—we would *always* be young.

Our future was not just bright. It was incandescent. Our horizons were endless—assuming there were any visible horizons at all from where we were sitting.

And where we were sitting for oh so many years was the catbird seat. We craved everyone's attention, and we got it. The opportunities were boundless. The sky was the limit, and we were too preoccupied with how special we were to even glance in that direction.

Fast forward half century or so. And that's not just an expression. If all these past decades don't seem like a blur to you, you must be on some miracle drug that stops the clock, and I'll have what you're having. Yes, the 1970s and 1980s seem like only yesterday, and no, they were not.

Social Security. Medicare. Problems with body parts you didn't know you had, treated by teams of specialists you didn't know existed. Retirement, early or delayed, voluntary or otherwise. Middle-aged children. And grandchildren already hurtling toward that age that we were when our own possibilities seemed endless.

But none of this was imaginable to us back in our youth. As to what lay ahead some six decades away, who knew?

As it happens, Simon & Garfunkel knew.

Paul Simon and Art Garfunkel, friends since elementary school, were a folk-rock duo who sold more than 100 million records. During the late 1960s and early 1970s, they recorded numerous iconic songs such as *The Sound of Silence*, *Scarborough Fair*, *Bridge Over Troubled Water*, and—my personal favorite—*The Dangling Conversation*. They won ten Grammy Awards and were inducted into the Rock and Roll Hall of Fame in 1990.

In 1968, they released an album called "Bookends." The track from that album that is perhaps best remembered, and—it seems—most often played on "oldies" radio stations, was *Mrs. Robinson*. Yes, *that* Mrs. Robinson—the seductress played by Anne Bancroft in the movie "The Graduate."

But a single line from another track from the "Bookends" album haunted me back in 1968 and it haunts me still. The song is called *Old Friends,* and it paints a picture of two elderly gentlemen sitting on a park bench "like bookends." We then hear this refrain:

"How terribly strange to be 70…."

How could they possibly know? How insightful for a couple of guys from Queens who were only about 27 years old at the time.

How terribly strange it has turned out. And how terribly strange how on the money those two guys were. How terribly strange indeed.

Let those of us who have crossed that threshold, and those who have plans to do so, explore together just how terribly strange it has all turned out. Let us try to figure out who we've become and how—if at all—we fit into a world that becomes less recognizable every day. Let us use some of our rapidly diminishing marbles to decode some of the mysteries of how creatures of the mid-20th Century can at least remain visible, if perhaps no longer all that relevant, in the 21st. And while we're at it, let's even celebrate our good fortune to have this opportunity to look backward and forward when so many of our contemporaries didn't live long enough to confront the mostly high-class problems we are now facing.

As it turns out, and as we will see, sometimes "terribly strange" equates to strangely terrible. And, fortunately, sometimes it does not.

CHAPTER 2

STRANGE AS IT SEEMS

To get a sense of how strange it is to be over 70 years old, it will be useful to establish a baseline as to what exactly constitutes strangeness. To that end, let us consider strangeness in the context of a random life-altering event that most of us have gone through one or more times: changing jobs.

Imagine you are about to report to your new job after many years in your prior position. You've already relocated to a new city, which is a pretty big change in and of itself. You want to get off on the right foot, so you give yourself lots of time to get to work on that first day.

You've scoped out the location of your new office on a map and determined that it is close to a particular subway stop. It looks like you have to change trains at one point, and you plan to do so. But when you get to that transfer point, you find that you need to walk almost a half mile to make the switch, and you start to get a little anxious about the time. *Damn—this looked easier on paper.*

On the second train, you stand up and get ready to detrain at your chosen station, but guess what: it's a local station, you're on an express train, and you hurtle past your stop. You need to backtrack (which you do) and you need to do it quickly (which you don't). *I wouldn't say I'm lost, but . . . .*

You know the address of your new office is 547 Main Street. You make your way to Main and find only 546 and 548. Shoot! . . . . *Wrong side of the street. . . .* You start to cross, and you worry that you're getting later and later, so you don't wait for a green light and . . . *Whew! Close call.*

You again start looking for 547 Main Street, and the odd numbers skip from 543 to 549. *Huh!* You swallow your pride and ask a passerby where 547 is, and you learn that the entrance is around the corner on a cross street. "Everyone knows *that,* pal." *Not me, "pal."*

You rush into the building as little beads of sweat are forming on your brow. You ask about your new company at the information desk, and you're told it's on the 33rd floor. You look for an elevator bank that serves, say, floors 31 through 40, but can't find one. You can't because it's one of those new-fangled buildings where you input your desired floor, the elevators confer among themselves, and decide which one will come for you. One does come, but you're too discombobulated to get on, and it leaves without you. So you try it again.

Are you getting the picture here?

You get off the elevator and go to the reception desk. There are three people there, and you don't know who to approach. They are chatting with each other with no indication that they plan to acknowledge your presence in the foreseeable future. Suddenly, a pause and you mentally flip a three-sided coin, choose a receptionist, and identify yourself by name as a new employee. They check their papers and computers and inform you that they have no record of anyone with your name scheduled to start work that day. *Could I have gotten the date wrong? Or did I change my name and forget to tell them?*

You give them the name of the person who interviewed you and ultimately made you the offer. "Sorry . . . she was transferred to our Memphis office last week. Is there someone else who would be expecting you?" *Well . . . no.*

Then the receptionist tries to call the assistant who used to work for your now-departed boss, but she finds that he's out sick. She finally finds another assistant who is tied up at the moment, but who agrees to come by in 10 minutes. Twenty minutes later, he comes to meet you. He knows nothing about your hiring, but he assures you that there is a team meeting in five minutes and perhaps it will get sorted out then. He doesn't know where you were supposed to have your office, so he takes you to a cubicle which may or may not be already occupied, so you can drop off your coat. *A cubicle? For this I gave up a corner office?*

You get led into a conference room where eight others are chatting and getting ready to begin a meeting. They seem to be speaking English, but nothing they say seems to make sense. Introductions are made, but it happens so quickly that you don't process a single name, let alone the pecking order. *OK . . . I must be the only person in this entire company who hadn't met a single soul here until this morning.*

The meeting goes on until close to noon. You have nothing to contribute because nothing they discussed rings any bells for you. At the end, it's agreed that you will work on a certain project. You don't have the foggiest idea what that project is, what your role is to be, or who to ask, or where to look it up.

The meeting breaks up, and as the group disperses, someone says, "Let's grab lunch at Freddie's." You never heard of Freddie's; you don't know where it is; and you don't know what time everyone plans to meet. It's not even clear that you've been invited. *What if I just want to sit in my cubicle and throw up?*

No, surviving in your 70s may not be as strange as this scenario. But strange it is, in its own way. Let's look at some of the ways. Consider this "day in the life" of a 70 plus senior citizen.

You wake up *way* too early. You've never been a good sleeper, but 5:30 a.m.? Really?

You look in the mirror, and it never fails to shock. Let's face it: you pick up a lot of wear and tear in 70 years. It's a good thing you haven't put on your glasses, for when you do, you're *really* in for it.

You take your morning meds, which are not to be confused with your bedtime meds. Over the years, you've accumulated an impressive array of pills you need to take daily. As it turns out, one of them is running low. You call the pharmacy and learn that you're out of refills, and they have to contact your doctor. They say they will. Maybe they will, and maybe they won't. You'll forget that you ordered the refill; but if it hasn't come when you're down to one or two pills, you'll remember to panic. This should not be confused with the panic you experience an hour after waking up, when you can't remember if you've already taken your morning meds or not. Skip the statin and risk a heart attack? Or take another and maybe risk an overdose?

You want to read the morning paper, and you think you're cool because you read parts of it on your iPad. But you really don't trust the electronic versions because they seem to be missing some of the good articles. So you get the print edition delivered; but it doesn't come until 7:00, and remember: you've been up since 5:30. So you start reading on your iPad. When the print version arrives, you start from scratch and notice that some of the articles seem strangely familiar. *I could swear I read this before.* (You did—about an hour ago on your iPad.)

If you are still working, you drive to the office. You walk to your workspace through a sea of people young enough to be your children—or even younger. If they look at the old person walking by at all—and most of them do not—they react with fear if you're a head honcho, or indifference (with a touch of pity) if you are not (and you most certainly are not).

You leave work and drive to the pharmacy on the way home to pick up that refill. Your driving leaves much to be desired, if your fellow motorists are to be believed. Through horns, glares, and the occasional middle finger, they make it clear that you are going too slow; that you are drifting in and out of your lane; and that your keys should be confiscated immediately.

You arrive at the pharmacy and pull into the nearly empty parking lot. You carefully pull into a space and go in to pick up your prescription. As luck would have it, there is no snafu with your Medicare Part D. You head back to your carefully parked car and discover that it is parked at about a 40 degree angle from the white lines and about 20% of your car is in an adjacent space. As you're getting into your car, some guy in the parking lot calls out "hey mister" and you realize it's you that he's calling. Seems you picked up a case of bottled water in the pharmacy, placed it on the bottom of your cart, and then just left it there—which is just as well, since you neglected to pay for it.

You head home and start to scare up something to eat. You blithely ignore the fact that your pantry is filled with food items that were "Best If Used" during the Bush administration. On those occasions when your kids have called you out on this, you proudly point out that at least it was Bush II! If you go out to eat, a quick scan of the restaurant makes clear that you're the oldest person in the place, including the owner, the employees, and all the other patrons. But you're accustomed to this, as it's been true for some 20 years.

We could go on—and we will in subsequent chapters. For now, let's just agree that getting old—and anyone over 70 is old by any standard—is sort of a *Twilight Zone* version of real life. It is a parallel universe that resembles life before 70 but differs in important ways. Not necessarily terrible or even bad, but terribly strange, nonetheless.

CHAPTER 3

OUR STRANGELY MIDDLE-AGED CHILDREN

A funny thing happened on the way to our 70s.

Actually, quite a few funny things happened and continue to happen as we slog through our eighth decade. We've already mentioned a few here and will be mentioning many more.

Some of those funny things are things *we* did, and others are things that just happened to *us*. We may think of some as being funny, while others might view them as sad, pointless, boring, or even pathetic. To each his or her own.

But all of the funny things that took place as we approached and passed 70 weren't necessarily about *us*. As baby boomers, we are of course accustomed to thinking that *everything* is about us. Objectively speaking, we know that isn't true—at least that's what we feel obliged to say.

If we are truly forced to look outward beyond ourselves, the first place our collective gazes might well land is our own children, nieces, nephews, and their contemporaries. Yes, a funny thing has happened to *them* when, perhaps, we weren't paying sufficient attention.

Turns out, they stopped being children. And yes, they stopped being young.

What they started to be is middle-aged.

I will be alluding in these pages to a celebration birthday dinner I attended with my family at the very moment the Coronavirus Pandemic of 2020 was about to come crashing down in mid-March of that year. The celebration was to honor my twin daughters. They had just turned 40.

You may be tempted to say that age is just a number. Or, 40 is the new 30. (Or is it, 50 is the new 40?) Let us not declare our kids middle-aged just because they have lived four decades. Let us instead examine the state of their lives today and see what it tells us.

My daughters are both married. I suppose that's typical, and in their case, pretty terrific. But it means that for at least a decade or so, I have not been the most important man in their lives. I get that, and I even celebrate that. But let's agree that a degree of separation from one's parents is a legitimate marker for middle age.

Here's another: children of their own. My daughters each have two, with their eldest now entering sixth grade. Their schedules are bewildering, if not mind-boggling, what with school, activities, play dates, birthday parties, what have you. The lives of their younger siblings may be a tad less complicated—or not. Another sign of middle age? Check.

Then there are our children's careers. By the time they are 40, if all goes well, they are settled into jobs and careers, and they have to navigate the often-treacherous waters of the workplace every day. Another check.

Because they have young children, and because they have jobs, they also have to deal with childcare. Is having an employee a sign of middle age? You bet.

And one more thing. They are now what was sometimes called the "sandwich" generation, placed midway between high-maintenance children and aging parents who may need a bit of maintenance, or even a lot of maintenance, or will need it sometime soon.

All of this takes place all the time in the lives of my kids. But when something like a pandemic comes along, everything in their lives got thrown for a loop. Working from home. On-line schooling. Play dates on FaceTime. Birthday parties on Zoom. Summer camps cancelling their seasons. Aging parents—i.e., us—at a high risk of the virus. Can you really think of the people who have to navigate all this as *children*?

When I listen to one of my daughters describe the juggling and maneuvering that often takes place in a single day of their lives, I get exhausted. I cannot imagine that I ever handled what's on their plate when I was 40.

Which brings us to what is perhaps the single strangest thing about my kids becoming middle-aged. I believe I must have gone through all of that middle age craziness myself back when I was 40. I know I had kids who juggled school, activities, play dates, and all that. I know I must have depended on lots of different people for childcare. I know I had parents back then who I had to worry about from time to time. On some level, I know all of this.

I just can't seem to remember it anymore.

CHAPTER 4

LITTLE STRANGERS

Perhaps the strangest thing of all about old age is this. In the grand scheme of things, the fates or the gods or maybe just random luck, or whoever or whatever determines how and when to hit us with good fortune or bad, have decided to save the best thing in life for last.

Yes, of course. We're talking about grandchildren, the one thing in life that, decidedly, is not overrated.

I will not pull any punches here. If you're of the view that rug rats should be seen and not heard—or maybe neither seen nor heard—I am not a kindred spirit. If you think these tykes are imperfect human beings, waiting in the on-deck circle to become as flawed as their parents—or, even worse, as awful as we are—look elsewhere for reinforcement. If you think grandkids are less interesting than your next golf game, or current events, or your latest visit to one of your doctors, or anything else, include me out.

We have already alluded to how decades have seemed to fly by, at ever greater velocities, on our way to 70 and beyond. For me, my 60s seemed to disappear in the blink of an eye. I'm now firmly convinced that this was because I was too busy falling in love with new grandchildren. Four of them, one at a time, starting shortly after my 63rd birthday and ending after my 68th. A girl, a boy, another girl, and then one more girl. Now and forever, four of the greatest people in my life.

Perhaps not coincidentally, I became a grandfather right around the time I was losing most of whatever passion I had for my profession. OK—maybe the passion was already long gone, and what I was losing was any residual interest in my day job. In any event, I was open to something that could consume me for a decade or two.

I must interject here that, on top of my incredibly good fortune in having a bunch of grandchildren, there was this bonus luck-out: my grandkids and their parents all live in the same metro area as do my wife and I. Unlike many of our friends, who need to get on a plane to visit their grandkids, for us it was just a car ride.

And so it came to pass that on a Thursday afternoon in the early days of the 2010s, when my first grandchild was a baby, I quietly left my office, drove to her neighborhood, and paid her a visit. Her parents were still at work, and her nanny had chores to take care of, so this little person and I had each other's undivided attention for maybe 45 minutes or an hour.

Thursday afternoon visits from grandpa started as a thing, then became a habit, and then an addiction. Sometimes my granddaughter would greet me gleefully; sometimes not. But I always headed home feeling glad that I had gone. I found myself making efforts to schedule business meetings, conference calls, and the like at any time other than Thursday afternoon. It became the highlight of my week, the perfect lead-in to the weekend, when I might spend even more time with my granddaughter, albeit not one-on-one.

My second grandchild made his appearance not long after the first. He lived in a different neighborhood from his older cousin, but I couldn't imagine making a Thursday trip without visiting him as well. So I didn't. I would now set out a bit earlier, drive to one of the kids' neighborhoods, park the car, visit, get back in the car, drive to the other neighborhood, park, visit, and head home. Eventually, the situation evolved into two *pairs* of grandkids to visit in different neighborhoods.

As time went on, the kids all got older and busier. Sometimes activities or illness made me skip a visit. For a time, due to scheduling conflicts (usually theirs, not mine), Wednesday became the new Thursday. But the tradition of grandpa visiting stretched on for a decade and beyond, until the coronavirus pandemic forced me to stop my visits.

Far be it for me to explain my strangely intense love for these kids. Instead, maybe I can at least express my fascination with them.

From the time they were infants, I've loved watching my grandkids observe their world. They look, they listen, you know they must be processing everything, and you wonder what it all means to them. I can't help but marvel at the process.

These little ones demonstrate their unique qualities almost from birth. Some of those qualities they get from their parents. Some of them seem to come directly from a grandparent, perhaps skipping a generation. And some of those qualities make them different from every other kid or person, and I can't help but marvel at that.

They have moods just like the rest of us. Sometimes on my weekly visits I was greeted as though I was the most important person on earth. Other times, I would walk in, and it barely registered that I was present. That bothered me not at all, because they may have had bigger fish to fry at that moment, as well they should.

One of the things I love about my grandkids is the way they seek out and bond with their peers. Perhaps my group is not representative, but here is the dynamic we have today. Grandchildren One and Two are close in age and are in the same grade at school. They have been cronies since they were babies. For a long time, when families got together and the adults would hug, so would One and Two. They seem to bring out the best in each other, and I can't get enough of watching them interact.

Grandchild Three is about two years younger than One and Two—more than enough to justify a difference in rank within the juvie hierarchy. Perhaps Three felt a bit excluded by the cliquishness of One and Two. So when Grandchild Four came along about two years after Three, Three made an executive decision. She declared herself in charge of all operations involving Four—who was happy to go along with that arrangement, especially when her big brother Two ditches his little sister Four for his crony, Cousin One.

In any event, I can't get enough of the Three/Four combo, sometime affectionately known as the J.V. On rare occasions, however, my grandkids will pair off in odd formations: One with Four and Two with Three; and precisely because it's so rare, I can't get enough of that either.

Sometimes, when all four of my grandchildren are together, the synergy really gets to me. During the late summer of the 2020 pandemic, they were all together having a blast in our backyard. At one point, they made an important announcement: they were forming a cousin's club. No surprise there; cousins do that a lot. What was surprising was their announcement that their youngest member, Grandchild Four, who was not yet five years old, had been elected president!

As much as I love watching my grandkids interact with their peers, I love even more how they want to play with *us*. It took me some time to figure this out, but until they are maybe five or six years old, they don't really appreciate how old and decrepit we grandparents are. They just lump us together with all other adults who are bigger and older than they are, without really understanding *how much* older we are, and what that means. When they ask us to play with them on the floor (which is easy enough), they think it's no big deal for us to keep getting up (which is no longer easy at all), then down again, then up once more, and so forth.

Another thing I love about my grandkids is their creativity. No, I don't mean to suggest that their work will win a Pulitzer or be hung at MOMA. I mean that when they are left to their own devices—preferably with another kid or two—they will pass on packaged games and make up games of their own. And they will compete with each other in these ragtag contests with an intensity that smacks of Game 7 of the World Series.

One of their creations I love the most isn't even really a game; it's a fort. Give a kid—or, better yet, a couple of kids—a blanket, and they will attach it to some odd piece of furniture and declare it to be a fort. And then they will declare you and any other adults to be *persona non grata*.

Yet another thing I love about my grandkids is that they seem to feel as at home in my house as I do. I spend more time visiting them than vice versa. But when they do drop in, they race off to obscure corners of my house and haul out playthings which I had long ago forgotten. And if conditions are right, they'll build a fort in my own home—and invite me to stay out.

When they do visit us and sleep over, I love the fact that, at least until they become adolescents, they are morning people—as am I. There is nothing like a well-rested young 'un or two, raring to go, with my morning coffee. Perhaps they're energized by the knowledge that, for at least a half a day or more, no one is going to make them go to bed. And nothing is more fun than serving them breakfast. One of them likes "Grandpa's granola"; one will eat anything so long as there is more than a trace of chocolate in it; one loves to *make* pancakes from scratch, but doesn't exactly love to *eat* them; and one has a thing for yogurt smoothies.

Because they get up early, there is always pressure for them to go to sleep at a reasonable time. Setting up is crucial: clocks; white noise makers; night lights; you name it. Then comes the fun part. I love how my grandkids scheme to stay up a little later and avoid having to actually sleep. Bathroom breaks. Missing toys, teddy bears, blankies, and other sleep necessities. Forgot to brush teeth. You and I couldn't make this stuff up. But they can.

I even love it when they fight with each other. The fights usually involve encroachment into someone's space, or misappropriation of someone's possessions. There is almost always a readily identifiable wrongdoer, who will eventually apologize. Sometimes those apologies are even sincere. Anger gets vented. But within hours or even minutes, all is forgotten, and life goes on. If only we adults could move on from tiffs this quickly as we go through life. (Ever watch a senior citizen hold a grudge? Not a pretty picture.)

We now must circle back to what is strange about all of this joy we (or at least I) get from grandchildren. Whenever seniors wax eloquently about their grandkids, someone will ask this: didn't your now-middle-aged children do all this cute stuff back in the day? Has your memory completely blanked out about what you were doing in your 30s and 40s?

Well, yes and no. Yes, because it's been quite a long while, and we've forgotten large chunks of everything. *Of course* we remember much about our kids growing up, including much that was wonderful.

But no because this is *different.*

The explanation I hear most often is that we were just too close to everything when we were raising our children. We were responsible for everything, every day; whereas grandparents get to pop in, have some fun, and go home to a quiet place.

But I'm not convinced it's that simple. I think it has something to do with the fact that our children are often too much like ourselves, and we often clash with them for exhibiting traits they received directly from us, wrapped up in a bow.

Not so with grandchildren! They may have bits and pieces of us, but that gets thrown in the genetic blender with good and bad stuff from a whole 'nother family. Our children are ours and ours alone, but we share our grandkids with other 70+ boomers—for better and for worse. So when one of our grandkids exhibits less than stellar behavior, we have plausible deniability. *"Didn't get that from me!"*

Perhaps the only way to test this theory is to live long enough to have great-grandchildren and retain enough marbles to appreciate what's happening. The gene pool for those tykes will be so diluted that any similarity between them and us will be purely coincidental.

And if that bit of good fortune comes my way, I will love those little strangers like there's no tomorrow.

CHAPTER 5

THAT TERRIBLE LOSS OF A SINGLE STEP

Several months into the 2020 Covid-19 pandemic, I decided to read "The Last Trial," the latest novel by Scott Turow. I have long been an ardent fan of Turow's legal fiction. And I will readily admit that I also have been hugely jealous of Turow's skills as a writer. I believe his ability to paint a picture of what goes on in a courtroom during a major trial is second to none.

"The Last Trial" brings Turow fans back to criminal defense attorney Alejandro (Sandy) Stern, an Argentina-born lawyer in Turow's fictional Kindle County, who had dazzled us Turow fans in earlier books. Stern is now over 80 years old. Along with his daughter and law partner Marta, and with some reluctance, he is now defending a scientist-cum-pharmaceutical executive who is accused in federal court of fraud, insider trading, and even murder, all involving a cancer drug.

I will not be giving away anything of substance to report that early in the trial, Stern stumbles. He makes a rookie mistake, and everyone in the courtroom knows it: Marta; the judge; the prosecutors; and especially Stern himself. Stern knows to a certainty that his younger self would never have made this blunder. The incident cannot but cause Stern to wonder, *have I lost a step? Am I just plain too old to be doing this anymore?*

The fictional Sandy Stern, of course, is considerably older than those of us who are now navigating the terrible strangeness of being over 70. But most of us have already lost a step or two at this point. Things are always changing in most businesses and professions, not to mention life in general. Keeping up can be difficult. Our younger colleagues often find it easier to adjust to new circumstances, and the temptation to rely on them can be irresistible. Much of what we do is more of a marathon than a sprint, but if we think we have the stamina we had twenty or thirty years ago, we're kidding ourselves.

In fairness, the fictional Sandy Stern was keenly aware of all this when he decided to take on the case in question. He had decided that this would be his last trial ever, and to make sure it was, he and Marta—no spring chicken herself—had arranged to shut down their law practice once this trial was at an end.

As it happens, the author Scott Turow himself turned 70 around the time he published "The Last Trial." And I am happy to report that, in my opinion, Turow has not lost any steps at all. His descriptions of all the dynamics that play out in a courtroom remain priceless. When a witness stretches the truth on the stand while Stern is cross-examining, we may get to see the silent strategizing that goes on between Stern and Marta as to how they should play it; the concerns of the prosecutors who may get up to object, but then have second thoughts; the reaction of the judge, who has been paying closer attention than we may have realized; the stirring among the jurors; and even the worried look on interested people in the gallery. To be sure, *my jealousy* over Turow's skills has lost no steps at all over the years.

I could not help but wonder if "The Last Trial" wasn't just the last trial for Stern and Marta, but also for Turow himself. In describing the physical and legal dismantling of the law firm of Stern & Stern, Turow has certainly closed the book on Sandy Stern. But Turow has created other fascinating characters in his three-plus decades writing fiction who we might like to revisit. And there are new characters waiting to be created. Whether or not Turow believes he has lost a step or two, a writer with Turow's abilities who may be shy a step or two can still spin a pretty good yarn. Which should remind all of us in our 70s that even if we lose—or have already lost—a step or two, the marathon is not yet over.

CHAPTER 6

THAT STRANGE PHENOMENON KNOWN AS FREE TIME

In 2020, two big things upended my life in a big way.

The first was personal: my phase-out from full-time work. It wasn't especially voluntary, and I wasn't particularly happy about it. I chuckle when I think back to times when I'd be with a friend and we'd see youngsters acting like jerks in a mall, or just otherwise being useless. I used to think I was being clever when I'd say to my friend, "I understand now why some species eat their young." It took me decades to learn how wrong I was. Turns out, in the business world, the species known as *homo sapiens* eats half of its elders for lunch and the rest for dinner. Who knew?

My change in status at work left me with the opportunity to continue to do some work on a part-time basis. But it soon became clear that this was mostly illusory. My younger former colleagues seemed convinced that my 46 years of experience wasn't all that useful, and so fewer and fewer tasks came my way.

The second big thing happened to the entire world: the Covid Pandemic. As discussed elsewhere, for a large chunk of 2020 we were mostly quarantined and locked down in our homes, and 2021 wasn't much better. Most of the workforce had to adapt to working at home. In my case, it was largely a matter of my *not* working from home.

I should interject here that for almost two decades I have had a daily commute of about an hour a day each way. Thus, whether I was working from home or *not* working from home, there were two more hours each day to fill.

All of this is by way of saying that starting in the early months of 2020, I had time on my hands. A lot of time. Much more than I had, say, even six months earlier. As this realization dawned on me, my first reaction was to fear that this was not going to be a pretty picture. I was never one for hobbies. I last played golf with any regularity—and no discernible skill whatsoever—in my 20s. This looked like it could get ugly.

Strangely enough, it did not.

Yes, I did watch a lot of television—as I always have. My wife and I have long enjoyed a lot of network dramas, and we still do. By late spring of 2020, the new episodes of network shows had gone into "hiatus." But by the middle of 2020, we were awash with more shows than we could handle on Amazon Prime, Netflix, and a gift subscription to Hulu. Still—surprisingly, at least to me—my TV consumption didn't increase all that much, if at all.

Yes, I also did some reading, as I always had. Much of it was when I climbed into bed, when I'd read a page or two and pass out. The next night I'd have to flip back a page or two to see where I left off, so my progress was a bit halting.

And yes, I have spent more time doing puzzles than I had for a very long time, a phenomenon that merits its own chapter.

I also ramped up my exercise regimen. For years while I was working full-time, I'd come home from work, hit the elliptical, grab some dinner, and shortly thereafter try—usually, with little success—to sleep. Now I found myself wanting to get my exercise over with in the morning, which I did.

But by dusk, and with the days getting longer, my wife started cajoling me into another session, usually a relaxed outdoor walk. My exercise life after 70 also merits its own chapter, but for present purposes let's just say that this was really just more of the same. Nothing new here.

It became clear that if I was going to be living with extra time on my hands, I was going to have to branch out a bit. And I did. Let's look at a few of the ways I found myself spending time.

I have always been averse to clutter. I grew up in a small apartment where, as it happens, the trash chute was right outside our door. My mother treated it like a kind of spare room. If something wasn't nailed down, down the chute it went.

One of my first activities during the pandemic was to do some decluttering. Of course, my home is a lot bigger than the apartment of my youth, and it would take my mother a lifetime to get rid of the flotsam and jetsam we've accumulated. Still, just making a start has been satisfying.

Here's one that you probably wouldn't have predicted. One day when I had little or no real work to do, my wife threw out this idea: become a math tutor! People pay good money to get help for their kids for the SAT. I could do it through FaceTime or whatever.

Now, I had been a pretty good math student—not great, but pretty good. I had taken five semesters of math at college. The only problem: that ended around 1966. How much could I possibly remember? To find out, I purchased an SAT prep book with loads of problems and their solutions. I worked my way through it as though I were going to take the SAT again. To my surprise, a lot of it came back. I wasn't sure if I was going to figure out how to launch this new career, but I discovered that I didn't care all that much. In a couple of months, I had rediscovered something that had brought me a lot of satisfaction in my youth. And I had retained a reasonable residuum of skills I had honed as an adolescent. Go figure. (Not long after this, many colleges decided to do away with requiring SAT scores. Oh well.)

As the cold and rainy spring of 2020 turned into summer, I turned my attention to the outdoors. When I first became a homeowner, I had my own lawn mower and I cut my own grass. Eventually, with heavy work schedules and young kids, that went by the wayside. But with time on my hands, I decided to tackle a few outdoor tasks. First, I realized that we needed mulch around our swing set and in some landscaping beds. This 73-year-old kid from the Bronx picked up the phone; had 25 bags of mulch delivered; toted them around the yard with the wheelbarrow he had last used during the Reagan administration; sliced them open with a box cutter (sorry, no blood to report here); and spread that stuff like he knew what he was doing.

I was so pleased with the result that I immediately dove into a related outdoor chore. Parts of my property were getting overgrown with weeds. I put on my old pair of gardening gloves and dove in, wondering if this is what George W. Bush meant by "clearing brush."

It wasn't. And it only took about two days for the poison ivy to blossom all over my unprotected arms.

At about this time, I was feeling badly about the inability of my then nine-year-old grandson to play all the sports he loved so much, due to the Covid-19 pandemic. I decided to order one of those outdoor basketball goals that you see on driveways all around the suburbs. It arrived in a box that I could not lift. The bags of nuts, bolts, and other hardware alone weighed as much as my grandson's little sister.

But I fearlessly set out to assemble this sucker. How could I not? People would point out that I had a degree in mechanical engineering, so how hard could it be? (Actually, I have *two* degrees in mechanical engineering; and still the answer was: hard as hell.) You'll love this, though: I actually got to the last step, involving the simple insertion of a six-inch-long bolt into holes with a three-eighths-inch diameter, and discovered that the only bolt I had left had a diameter of a half inch. I had apparently used the skinny bolt in one of the first steps of the assembly, where a fatter bolt had been called for. So it was either disassemble the whole monstrosity, or pop over to the local hardware store and buy a skinny bolt. (Strangely, only $2!)

There is this one last thing I did with some of my newfound free time: I started this book. I had self-published two earlier books and had gotten a huge kick out of it each time. Back then, I put pressure on myself to come up with topics for new chapters. Now, I could wait for inspiration, and—sooner or later—it would seem to come.

So, you may be wondering, how did this turn out? I can't say for sure, but I can assure you of this:

You'll be the first to know.

CHAPTER 7

THE STRANGELY LASTING ALLURE OF PUZZLES

Strangely enough, as it turns out, you *can* teach an old dog new tricks. Or at least an old baby boomer. Or maybe it's just a certain species of baby boomer and a certain type of trick.

I grew up watching my father solve crossword puzzles. At the time, growing up in New York City, there were six or more daily newspapers, and most of them offered a daily crossword puzzle. Some of them were less than challenging, so my father gravitated toward the puzzles in the *New York Times.* He would fold the paper up so he had something to lean on—which he needed because he always did the puzzle in pen. Yes, that could be presumptuous, though he had mastered the art of entering his less certain answers with varying degrees of faintness.

Before long, I was doing them as well. As an adult, when I commuted by train or bus, I would tackle the crossword every day. Then, for many years, I drove to work, so I mostly worked on Sunday puzzles—the big ones with the clever themes. And, yes, I did them in ink—with some answers bold, some answers starting out faint—and often wrong.

Over time, I branched out a bit. The Sunday *Times* magazine has long offered a "variety" puzzle each week in addition to the traditional crossword. One such variety was called Pun & Anagrams, which used a standard crossword-type grid, where the "pun" clues had you groaning, and the "anagram" clues had you scrambling.

From there, around my 50s or 60s, the natural progression took me to Cryptic puzzles. These use a grid that is sort of a skeletal version of a traditional crossword, in which—unlike traditional crosswords—there are some squares you can fill only with an across word or a down word, but not both. The clues mixed the traditional with wordplay, and they were never easy. I would often keep returning to it for the entire week. Sometimes I would get the right words without even knowing how they related to the clue. Still, fun and challenging.

As I got into my 60s, I got a little more ambitious, taking on the much-feared Diagramless puzzle. This was just like a traditional crossword, except there were no black squares in the grid. You had to figure out where they went. The *Times* would tell you what type of "symmetry" the grid exhibited—if any. It would also offer the helpful bit of information as to where 1-Across started; but because some purists didn't want to be contaminated with this hint (I was not one of them), they hid that information on another page. Over time, I got pretty good at these, though I learned early on that if I could not solve 1-Across, I might as well pack it in.

Over the years, I had dabbled in Acrostic puzzles, but never became a big fan. Acrostics have a grid which, when completed, spells out an insightful paragraph from a book. To fill the grid, you have to guess the answers to about two dozen clues, and then move the letters from those completed clues into designated spaces on the grid. Often, those clues were just too obscure for me. I found the process boring and often bailed without a solve.

By around my mid-60s, I realized something about Acrostics: the "tipping point." Once you figured out a decent number of the clues, you could see words forming in the grid. When you filled in the missing letters of those words, you could then export those letters back into clues you hadn't yet solved. There would come a point—and it varied from Acrostic to Acrostic—when you could see how words that were already formed in the grid could be combined with other words into full sentences. And then the solutions to the unsolved clues would start to cascade until the rest of the puzzle got done in a flash—often after a *very* slow start.

I came to enjoy the tipping point so much that if I couldn't solve enough clues honestly to get there, I would brazenly cheat until I arrived at the tipping point. There it is. Full confession.

All of this is by way of a preview of how this old dog learned some new tricks after turning 70. In 2020, the *Times* took pity on its readers being stuck in Covid quarantine at home and decided to freshen up the puzzle page of the daily print edition. In addition to some daily brainteaser, like a Cryptogram (which I had last seen in the New York *Herald Tribune* when that paper still existed), they began to offer a puzzle called "Two Not Touch."

This is a 10 by 10 grid broken up into regions of different sizes and shapes. The object is to place exactly two stars in each column, each row, and each region, but no two stars can touch one another. When I first tried it, I couldn't imagine how it could be done. So I found a tutorial on line, and learned that the key was not to figure out where the stars *go*, but rather where they *don't* go. You start with low hanging fruit like, say, a horizontal region that is only three squares wide and one square high. Since that region must have two stars, they must go in the two ends or else they would touch. That lets you eliminate the middle square in that region, as well as all other squares that abut one or both of the stars, and all other squares in that horizontal row. And so forth.

I eventually got pretty good at this. And I also got addicted. I would get the morning paper, rush through most of it, and then tackle the pair of Two Not Touch puzzles offered ever day but Sunday. But some of them were just too darn hard. I would sit there and stare, waiting for some insight, and none would come. Other times, I got so overconfident that I ripped through them really quickly, only to discover that I had made a fatal mistake early on by placing a star in the wrong square, or prematurely eliminating a square when it wasn't warranted. Because I had—of course—done it in ink, there was no going back. Add one to the loss column.

After a year or so, I got into a steady state. I was solving maybe 90% of the Two Not Touch puzzles. But in late 2021, I discovered a trick one day which allowed me to solve what seemed like a hopelessly difficult puzzle. And I found that this trick could help me on quite a few subsequent puzzles. Chalk up another new trick for the old dogs.

As the Covid pandemic of 2020 ground on into autumn, there were days when I had completed (or not) the traditional crossword and completed (or not) both Two Not Touch puzzles, and I still wasn't feeling satisfied. I started to eye the one daily puzzle that had never appealed to me very much: Ken Ken. Like Two Not Touch, it had a grid divided into regions, but now you had to come up with a specified number through a specified mathematical operation: addition, subtraction, multiplication, or division. Each row and column had to use each digit once and only once. In the baby version on which I would cut my teeth, which was 4 by 4, each row and column had to have a 1, a 2, a 3 and a 4.

I started tacking these suckers by trial and error—in ink, of course. I would quickly run into problems and get frustrated. I had to keep crossing out numbers in those small spaces and trying a different number, to the point that most or all of the sixteen squares were filled with discarded digits. So, once again, I sought out and found a tutorial online, and discovered that I'd do better if there was a method to my madness. By the winter of 2020-21, I had gotten pretty proficient in the 4 by 4, and I started to try the daily 6 by 6. By the summer of 2021 I was able to solve the 4 by 4 almost every day, and a respectable percentage of the 6 by 6 puzzles. By the end of 2021, I was solving more than half of the 6 by 6 puzzles. By late March of 2022 I solved an especially easy 6 by 6 in just over three minutes. In April 2022, I solved my first 7 by 7. The one certainty I face every day is a bunch of squares with lots of numbers—in ink, of course—with many of them crossed out.

You may be wondering why I haven't said much about those Cryptograms that the *Times* offers twice a week. When they first appeared in the early days of the pandemic in 2020, I tried a few and actually solved a couple. But then came weeks in which I couldn't make a dent in them. This is not surprising, since I'd never really tried to be strategic about them. For the most part, my only trick was to look for one-letter words which I knew had be "a"s or "I"s, which rarely got me very far. Two years later, in 2022, I gave them another shot and tried a few other things. For example, if there was an apostrophe before the last letter, it was probably an "s" or a "t." And if a word had two of the same letters together, there were certain letters which they *couldn't* be, such as "h," "j," "q," and so forth. I started to have success on the Cryptogram maybe once a month—or maybe not. Will I ever get good at them? I will let you know if I do; but if you don't hear from me, write this off as an unsuccessful project.

By now you might be wondering: what about Wordle? This is the word game the *Times* began to offer online in 2022, and it quickly became the rage. It reminded me of Jotto, an old game played with paper and pencil (yes, pens worked here too), where you guess at your opponent's secret word and learn how many letters the two words share. Then your opponent tries to guess your own secret word. This continues until one of you figures out the other's secret word.

Wordle is different. When you guess at the secret word, you learn *which* letter or letters they share. You also learn which letters of the secret word share the same position as in your word, and which appear elsewhere. And you only get six guesses. No, this is not your grandpa's Jotto.

So here's my first epiphany: strange as it may seem, it *is* possible to learn something new after 70. We are not consigned to the same skill set we had for most of our lives. Some life-long skills might fray or even leave us for good; but others can be acquired, even by people our age.

A second epiphany: I've long realized that if a crossword puzzle has you stumped, put it aside and come back to it. With fresh (or refreshed) eyes, you often can make a breakthrough. But now that I have more time on my hands, I can put puzzles aside for days or even a week. And this strategy seems to work with other puzzles like Two Not Touch and Ken Ken.

On the other hand, here's one more thing I *haven't* learned in 70+ years of solving puzzles, but perhaps there's still hope:

Try using a pencil, hot shot.

Alas, we're not quite done with the subject of puzzles. In the Spring of 2022, I had occasion to be hanging out with my eleven-year-old granddaughter while I was bouncing from puzzle to puzzle in the weekend paper. My granddaughter has always had a thing for puzzles, so I took the opportunity to introduce her to Two Not Touch. It took her about five minutes to understand the rules. By around the fifteen-minute mark she was having the types of insights that had taken me months and scores of prior puzzles to come up with. After a while we switched to Ken Ken and started with the weekend 5 by 5 version. Once she knew the rules, she figured that one out, dove directly into the 7 by 7 version, and sussed out a big chunk of it.

So I would like to offer a corollary to the notion that old dogs can learn new tricks. It may explain why many employers show seniors to the door to make room for someone fifty years younger.

Young pups can learn new tricks as well. And they can do it faster, and maybe even better, than us old dogs.

CHAPTER 8

THE STRANGE POTENCY OF DISTANCE

In around 1961, I was hanging out at my best friend's home on a Sunday afternoon. His family made it a practice of having a traditional Sunday dinner, and they were kind enough to invite strays like me to join them. That particular Sunday I accepted their offer, and I learned something that gets driven home again and again, the older I get.

My friend's dad was an erudite gentleman who liked to engage in provocative discussions about current events, politics, and the like. So there was nothing particularly unusual about my friend and I chattering at the dinner table about the latest comings and goings of the youthful Kennedy administration and what it liked to call the "New Frontier." I don't recall what exactly we said, but the message my friend's dad received was that we believed the changes that were happening in America at the time would permanently alter politics and society.

After hearing what we had to say, my friend's dad leaned back in his chair and smiled. I'm not sure if he thought we were just young, naïve, or both. But I remember well what he actually said.

He explained that political and other forces act like a pendulum in an old grandfather clock. When things go too far in one direction, or for too long, a sort of self-correction kicks in, and things move back toward the center—and beyond. They may then go too far in that opposite direction, and then the pendulum swings again, back to the original direction.

It didn't take too long for my friend and I to witness this in real time. The progressive initiatives of the abbreviated Kennedy presidency and the Johnson administration which followed had sown the seeds of Richard Nixon's political rebirth. Nixon had lost to Kennedy in the close 1960 election and had then suffered the embarrassment of losing a race for governor of California in 1962, prompting him to say that we wouldn't have Nixon to kick around anymore. Turns out we would, and we did, when he ran for president a second time in 1968, but he delivered more kicks than he received, eking out a narrow victory over Hubert Humphrey.

Perspective. That is what my friend's dad had in large supply, while my friend and I—teenagers—had almost none. He had been born around the First World War, and had lived through the Great Depression, World War II, and the Korean War. He had seen presidents come and go. He was able to take the long view of things because he had already lived through much. More importantly, he had always paid attention.

I suppose I still remember that exchange at dinner around 1961 because I am fortunate that this particular friendship has continued over these many decades. Through those years, whenever we seemed to be heading into a watershed election, my friend and I would check in with each other with a quick text or e-mail, along the lines of "Q: Pendulum about to swing? A: Yup."

I mention all this because in the 2020s, as we navigate the oddity of being over 70, *we* are now—strangely enough—the folks with perspective. Who else but us codgers can remember when the Republican Party could produce a California governor and U.S. Supreme Court Chief Justice named Earl Warren? Does anyone else remember when seemingly pointless and virtually endless foreign wars were fought not by volunteers but by draftees, and avoided by those who ran to Canada, claimed to be a conscientious objector, failed the army physical, or just lucked out in a draft lottery? People who are now, say, younger than 50 have no recollection of great moments like the first moon landing, or national tragedies like the assassinations of the 1960s.

Yes, the perspective one gains from old age extends from the important down to and beneath trivialities. Every now and then, when a youngster (i.e., someone aged 15 to 59) complains about a cell phone dropping a call, I am quick to hijack the conversation to relate how, back in the day, a phone was a heavy black box hardwired to a wall, or something into which you fed nickels and dimes at an airport. Buffering problem while streaming a program on Amazon Prime? Back in the day, we had only six channels, no cable, blah, blah, blah.

Still, real perspective was especially valuable in the age of Donald Trump. We often read and hear pundits say that Trump isn't any worse than Nixon and other presidents who presided over disastrous events, manmade and otherwise. To those who say that I say you must not be over 70; but if you are, for all these decades, you probably haven't been paying attention.

And as the 2020 election approached, I couldn't help but wonder: is there still a pendulum and does it still work? The answers we got in November 2020: yes, and yes—albeit barely. It wasn't until January 6, 2021, that I began to wonder whether an angry mob could destroy not only the pendulum, but the entire clock and the whole democratic superstructure that allows voters to push pendulums in one direction or the other.

CHAPTER 9

THE STRANGELY DELICIOUS ABILITY TO SAY WE KNEW THEM "WHEN"

I suppose everyone who watches television or movies has had this experience. An actor appears on screen, perhaps unexpectedly, and the viewer recognizes them, or at least thinks they do. If the actor has been visible on a continuous basis for some time, the mere recognition is no big deal. But if the actor has not been seen for some time, the viewer may well notice, for the first time, that—surprise! —the actor has aged a bit. Fun, but again no big deal.

What is more interesting, at least to me, is when we see an actor who has been out of the public eye for years or even decades. The actor may now be an older version of their younger self or may have changed to the point of becoming unrecognizable. But a sighting like this can provoke an irresistible urge to tell your fellow viewers, "I remember her from way back when she was a regular on. . . ."

Of course, the older one gets, the larger the universe of old-time actors that can be spotted and identified in current films and programs. Those of us in our 70s were the first TV generation. We have been watching TV and movies for some six decades, so there are an awful lot of screen personalities to remember. Of course, remembering celebrities—or anything else—is not really our strong suit these days. So, it can be strangely delicious to spot someone in a current TV show and cry out, "Yes!!! She was a nurse on *ER*!" or "Wasn't he that sleazy cop on *Hill Street Blues*??"

During the 2020 Covid Pandemic, I had an opportunity to wallow in the past while revisiting some young and talented people—all from the same TV show—who did great work in the 1980s and went on to really knock people's socks off for years and even decades, right up to the present. My family gave me a gift subscription to Hulu, a streaming service that seems to maintain a huge inventory of old TV shows. One of them was one of my absolute favorite shows of all time: *St. Elsewhere.*

St. Elsewhere was not the first medical drama series on TV, nor the last. It ran for six seasons, from the fall of 1982 to the spring of 1988. It was set in a city hospital called St. Eligius in a poor section of Boston. Like earlier medical shows, it featured a group of experienced senior physicians, played by Ed Flanders, Norman Lloyd, and William

Daniels. They were fine performers, but *St. Elsewhere* was arguably the high point of their careers.

Not so for the rest of the cast, who played medical residents, nurses, and other hospital personnel. As I rewatched episode after episode in 2020, I was amazed how often their early TV personas proved to be predictors of what we would see when they became boldfaced names decades later.

Before we get to them, it's worth mentioning one young actor who had already achieved a bit of stardom before *St. Elsewhere.* **Stephen Furst** played Elliot Axelrod on *St. Elsewhere*, a medical student who became a resident later on. He was a chunky and klutzy worry wart who ricocheted from one hospital crisis to another. But he was already well known to that segment of immature American males who, if pushed, will admit that their favorite movie *ever* was *National Lampoon's Animal House.* In that 1978 movie about fraternity antics, Furst had played Kent Dorfman, a/k/a Flounder, a chunky and klutzy pledge who spent much of the movie worrying about his brother's car which the frat boys hijacked for their infamous "road trip" and later turned into a homecoming parade float.

If you will allow me one more preliminary digression, let us also consider **Eric Laneuville**. He played Luther Hawkins, the diminutive hospital orderly at St. Eligius, and was one of the only actors in the opening credits who didn't play a doctor or a nurse. Yet his outsize character seemed to play a central role in any and all shenanigans at the hospital, or efforts to undo the damage caused by other flake outs. But Laneuville's talents weren't limited to acting. By 1984, he was directing episodes of *St. Elsewhere*, including episodes in which he also appeared as Luther Hawkins. If I've done the math correctly, he would have been about 32 years old at the time. He went on to direct episodes of countless TV shows including *L.A. Law*, *Quantum Leap*, *NYPD Blue*, *Monk*, *Blue Bloods*, *Agents of S.H.I.E.L.D.*, *Chicago Fire*, *A Million Little Things*, *Lethal Weapon*, and *NCIS: Los Angeles*.

So, who else are you likely to see on TV or in movies that got a start—or a boost—on *St. Elsewhere*? If you're into comedy, you're probably familiar with **Howie Mandel**. He created a children's cartoon series; achieved fame as a stand-up comedian; hosted game shows; and served as a judge on *America's Got Talent*. But few of his current fans—and perhaps none of his younger fans—are likely to remember Mandel's role as Dr. Wayne Fiscus on *St. Elsewhere*. If a group of medical residents could have a class clown, Fiscus was it at St. Eligius.

If you're more into drama today, you are surely familiar with **Mark Harmon**. From 2003 through 2021, he played Special Agent Leroy Jethro Gibbs on *NCIS*, a dour, intense investigator who brooked no nonsense from his underlings. If you happened to watch him during his three seasons on *St. Elsewhere*, that will ring a bell—at least at first. He played plastic surgeon Dr. Robert Caldwell, who initially spent a great deal of time ejecting the buffoonish surgical resident Victor Ehrlich (played by **Ed Begley, Jr.**, who would also become a prolific actor and as recently as 2022 scored a recurring role in Better Call Saul) for making tasteless and disrespectful comments in the operating room. Harmon's uptight Gibbs-in-training character evolved into a bed-hopping lothario. He eventually went through a meltdown, had his handsome face slashed by a woman he met at a bar, and contracted AIDS.

And perhaps you have made the acquaintance of **Denzel Washington**. He has starred in numerous films, including *Malcolm X*, *Training Day*, *Fences*, *Antwone Fisher*, *The Equalizer*, and a personal favorite of this boy from the Bronx, *The Taking of Pelham 123*. He has won a Tony award, two Golden Globes, and two Academy Awards. In films, he often plays characters with a soft voice and laser-like intensity—which was visible during his six seasons on *St. Elsewhere*. There he played Dr. Phillip Chandler, one of the few residents who exuded competence and behaved professionally but was always acutely conscious of his race.

For a year or so of *St. Elsewhere's* run, **Alfre Woodard** played obstetrician Roxanne Turner. She was Denzel Washington's love interest, but—alas—he was not hers—until he was. When she left *St. Elsewhere*, she had a prolific career, earning countless nominations and awards, including Emmys for her work on *L.A. Law* and *The Practice*. In December 2020 the *New York Times* included Woodard in its list of the 25 Greatest Actors of the 21st Century (So Far), with a rank of 17. (Denzel? His rank was #1.)

And then there is **Helen Hunt**. You may remember her perky character in the sitcom *Mad About You*, for which she won Golden Globe and Emmy awards, or perhaps her portrayal of perky Carol Connelly in the romcom *As Good as It Gets*, for which she won an Academy Award. What you may not remember is her role in *St. Elsewhere* as Clancy Williams, the perky sometime girlfriend of the sad-sack widowed resident Dr. Jack Morrison (played by **David Morse**, himself, much later, an Emmy nominee for playing George Washington in the HBO miniseries *John Adams,* and the co-star of the Broadway show, *How I Learned to Drive,* which opened in 2022—fifty years after he first appeared on *St. Elsewhere*). Hunt's character brought Dr. Morrison back to life and then broke his heart by getting an abortion.

Of course, *St. Elsewhere*, like many scripted dramas, had numerous guest stars over the course of its six-year run. But none had a sufficiently lasting role to provide me with an "aha" moment when they turned up years or decades later. Which is why, perhaps, you *should* watch all six seasons now, even if you never missed one back in the 1980s. If you did, during the second and third seasons, you would see that there were a couple of story arcs involving a local TV producer who creates a documentary about St. Eligius, and then enlists Ed Begley's character to do a "health" spot on the evening news. The actor playing the producer is thin and dark haired, and comes across as a mix of sketchy, edgy and sleazy. He wouldn't have made much of an impression on me back in my late 30s. But he wasn't terribly strange, or strange at all, when I watched again in my 70s. It was **Michael Richards**—who would become a star a decade later, playing Kramer on the iconic comedy *Seinfeld*.

And if you are crazy enough to slog through *St. Elsewhere* up to its last seasons, as I did, you might be pleasantly surprised to see **Bruce Greenwood**, then 30 years old, appearing as a regular, playing young Dr. Seth Griffin, a wise-ass corner cutter who regularly gets himself and others into trouble. Greenwood is one of those solid performers that you know you've seen in a lot of stuff, though you sometimes forget his name. But I sure didn't. Since 2018, I had been enjoying him in yet another medical drama: *The Resident.* But now, 35 years later, he is no young doctor. While still a bit of a wise ass and a corner cutter, he was now Chief of Surgery and later became the CEO of his hospital. And one of his senior colleagues at his current TV hospital turns out to be someone else you may remember from the 1980s: **Malcolm-Jamal Warner**, who hit paydirt at the age of 14 playing Theo Huxtable on *The Cosby Show.*

My point here is not to convince you to watch *St. Elsewhere* if you never saw it in the 1980s, or even if you did, though you really should. It is just to illustrate how much fun it can be to recall the young versions of famous performers even as they now settle into roles as men and women of a certain (mostly old) age. Strangely enough, we can have more fun doing this than our kids precisely because we started watching movies and TV decades before they did. While it is true that we are losing our memory at an alarming rate, they say that long-term memory is more durable than short-term. If that is really true, perhaps you'd like to chat about *The Fugitive.*

So next time you binge on a *Netflix* series, or when you unearth an old movie that somehow got past you when it first came out, stick around when the credits roll. You never know when you might see an actor you knew back "when."

CHAPTER 10

NOSTALGIA, STRANGELY ENOUGH, IS EVEN BETTER THAN IT USED TO BE

We've all heard the line at one time or another. It is usually delivered to someone who is eloquently and wistfully talking about the so-called good old days. The line is a somewhat arch way of asserting that the person doing the reminiscing is looking backward through rose colored glasses. It is a line that many people believe—with good reason—to have originated with Yogi Berra.

"Nostalgia ain't what it used to be."

I have two quibbles with this, one large and one small. For the small one, it turns out that in this one rare instance, a bit of folk wisdom did not originate with Yogi. It was a slightly modified version of the title of a 1978 autobiography by an Academy Award winning French actress named Simone Signoret, "Nostalgia Isn't What It Used to Be."

My larger quibble is that she was wrong.

Ms. Signoret did not survive into her 70s, so her opportunities for nostalgia were, sadly, cut short. But those of us now in our 70s can wallow in memories of six full decades and more, and those earlier decades have now had a chance to fully marinate, erasing any recollection of any downside associated with those days of yore. And Ms. Signoret most assuredly did not live to experience the Covid pandemic of 2020-22, when the most mundane activities that preceded the pandemic became the grist for blissful memories, and our failure to fully appreciate them haunts us even now.

I have long been addicted to nostalgia. While my short-term memory is now as bad as, or even worse than, others in their 70s, my long-term memory seems to hang tough. And there are plenty of people who have been a part of my life for a very long time and who share those memories. I believe nostalgia is a team sport, best played with at least two people, and the more, the merrier. It only takes one old-timer to reminisce about the exaggerated wonders of days past, but it takes two or more to really blow such wonders out of all proportion.

For example, my oldest friend and I still love to talk about our days in junior high school. We might shmooze about the class clown or recall adolescent fantasies about certain teachers. Perhaps my wildest exaggeration is about my ninth grade general science teacher who, I will regularly insist, was the best science teacher I ever had (no small thing, since I later took years of biology, chemistry, and physics in high school and college). Of course, those fond memories of junior high always block out the fact that my school was in a rough neighborhood in the Bronx, and hardly a day went by from 1959 to 1961 that I wasn't shaken down for my lunch money by some young thug.

Then there was my best friend from summer camp. We spent the summers from 1955 through 1964 together and piled up memories galore. Years later, we would gab about how clever we were in psyching out when and how Color War would "break." (We never actually got it right.) Of course, our strolls down memory lane studiously ignored the fact that much of camp, and almost all of Color War, consisted of athletic competitions. And my buddy and I were always the last ones picked on teams when it was time to "choose up sides."

My wife and I reminisce often about the early days of our marriage in the 1970s and 80s. We will sometimes obsess about when our daughters were little girls and all the adorable things they did. Those memories usually crowd out any recollection about the crazy problems we had with childcare and all the times we had to change the locks on our house.

But now, with extra decades stacked between the present and those long-ago times, the bad stuff seems even more forgettable and the good memories more memorable. Simone Signoret was only 57 when she wrote her memoirs. Her most vivid memories would have been maybe 30 years old. For those of us climbing into our 70s, there is nostalgia material that is close to half a century old.

While Ms. Signoret sadly died at the age of 64, she might have felt differently about nostalgia had she lived through the Covid pandemic. For months through 2020 and beyond, my family, friends, and I have reminisced about the simple pleasures we enjoyed all the way back in 2019. A relaxed meal in a restaurant with old friends. A trip to the mall for a bit of shopping, a bite to eat, and maybe a movie. A trip to an out-of-town wedding or other function with a relaxing night in a hotel. A sporting event—*any* sporting event, from a major league baseball game down to my grandson's traveling soccer team. A birthday party for one of my grandkids at an arts and crafts place, complete with a birthday cake with candles that had to be blown out. A simple hug from any of my offspring. Even a routine visit to a doctor where you didn't have to worry about going home sicker than when you arrived.

What I've learned about nostalgia lately is that the good old days don't have to be all that old at all to create fond memories. We just need to hang on long enough to appreciate how good those days were and how much we have lost.

CHAPTER 11

THAT STRANGE, NOVEL, AND UNIMAGINABLY TERRIBLE VIRUS

For much of our 50s and 60s, the only types of viruses we were concerned about seemed to be those that threatened to consume our computers. In 2020 and 2021, and well into 2022, the world was consumed by a real virus: a deadly bug that sickened millions and killed hundreds of thousands in the United States alone. It was initially called the "novel" coronavirus, and the disease it inflicted was Covid-19. For those of us over 70, there was a somewhat novel, albeit dubious, distinction: we were considered to be at a high risk of infection and death.

The episode began as something that was barely on our radar screens. My own diary of the early months of 2020, before the world came crashing down, now seems in retrospect to have been strange in the extreme, if not altogether eerie.

My wife and I spent about five days in the middle of February at Disney World in Florida with our kids and grandkids. We took a crowded flight down to Orlando, from one crowded airport to another crowded airport, then a crowded Disney shuttle to a crowded Disney hotel. We spent about three days at teeming theme parks, with people from all over the United States and beyond, waiting on long lines and eating in crowded restaurants. We went home on another crowded shuttle to a crowded airport, onto a crowded plane, flying into another crowded airport.

As it happened, about five days after returning from Disney, I accompanied my wife to a professional conference in Atlanta. Another crowded flight to a teeming downtown hotel. Bustling meetings; dinners in crowded restaurants; and all that. At the end, another flight on a crowded plane from one crowded airport to another. We got home on Leap Day, February 29, 2020.

As the icing on the cake, on March 11, my wife took me for that most elective of all medical procedures—a colonoscopy!—at a hospital about 15 miles from Manhattan, which was by then the epicenter of the pandemic.

Thus, over the course of a month or so, we were in close physical proximity to *thousands* of people. And it only became clear after the fact that a goodly number of those poor souls must have been infected with Covid-19, whether they knew it, or we knew it, or not. The magnitude of what was happening was just about dawning when our family went out for a birthday dinner in Manhattan on the 40th birthday of my twin daughters in mid-March of 2020. I was surprised by what a great parking space I got on Fifth Avenue, around the corner from the restaurant, realizing only later that I was the only guy dumb enough to drive into the belly of the beast at that point. By the following Monday, we were in lock-down in what came to feel like a rubber room.

The weeks that followed in March and April gave new meaning to the term suspended animation. Hours glued to screens for work-related video conferences, followed by video sessions with kids and grandkids that invariably descended from silliness to chaos. Outdoor walks with face masks, constantly crossing streets to avoid other pedestrians and cyclists. (At the very beginning, I didn't even own a mask, so I tried to make a handkerchief into something like a bandana.) We would put on masks when we saw pedestrians approaching. But cyclists came our way too fast to do that, so I would hold my breath for about 10 seconds while the cyclist whizzed by.

A fraught weekly trip to the supermarket, where plexiglass screens separated customers from cashiers; one-way aisles prevented face-to-face encounters; and many shelves were empty, week after depressing week. The 7:00 to 8:00 a.m. hour was reserved for us senior citizens and other high-risk folks, and we codgers began lining up around 6:50 a.m.

Things took an even stranger turn around May, when a vocal

and aggressive minority began badgering authorities to "reopen" the economy. The prospect of spreading the infection—when millions were struggling to maintain social distancing—didn't seem to faze these folks. They claimed their civil rights were being violated because they couldn't patronize "essential" businesses like tattoo parlors.

By June of 2020, a "second wave" of Covid-19 hit the United States—with a vengeance. While up to this point the virus seemed reasonably well contained in New York and nearby areas, it ballooned up in places that had rushed to "reopen," where precautions had not been followed all that strictly in any case. By this point, so many people were feeling like zombies. "Normal" life was becoming a distant memory.

Perhaps the saddest moment for me was the cancellation of summer camps. I had been a camp kid from 1955 to 1964, and I was excited that my two oldest grandkids had signed up enthusiastically for overnight camps, after a lengthy search that was not unlike the college selection process we had gone through with our children in the late 90s. While some camps figured out a way to make a go of the 2020 season, the two camps that my grandkids were planning to attend simply cancelled. Sad as this was, I was strangely grateful that it had played out this way. Had they stayed open, the parents would have had to make an awfully difficult decision. At least they were spared from having to choose between safety and trying to protect their kids from disappointment.

Spring gradually gave way to summer, but while the seasons did change, the situation didn't all that much. July was *hot,* but not hot enough to burn off the virus. The heat did, however, have some impact. For one thing, it apparently sent our local mice population scurrying for cooler quarters, and a select group of them found their way into our basement. The heat also put a strain on our air conditioners. One of them gave out, but it proved to be repairable, but another gave up the ghost altogether and had to be replaced.

July gave way to August, and the hits just kept on coming. Tropical Storm Isaias caused a huge amount of damage in our area. Many people lost power for as much as a week. We escaped that problem, but our cable and internet were knocked out for three days. Even a brief loss of cable is a big deal to a couple of TV addicts. In years past, we would have turned to DVDs; but we had migrated over to the world of streaming, which didn't depend on cable—but it did require Wi-Fi, and we didn't have any. The loss of Wi-Fi didn't just cramp our styles insofar as entertainment was concerned. Whatever work we were doing, we were doing it from home; and without Wi-Fi, we were without e-mail and we couldn't participate in meetings on Zoom and the like. Fortunately, our daughter taught us how to create hot spots with our cell phones, and to my astonishment, it actually worked! (I'll never understand how your cell phone can create a hot spot for another device to access Wi-Fi, but not itself.)

In the second week of August, I turned 73 and realized that almost half of my 73rd year had disappeared into a black hole.

By the fall of 2020, not much had changed. People in our orbit started to get together for take-out dinners on our suburban patios, and it seemed like a lovely bit of normalcy. As the weather cooled, people started shopping for outdoor heaters. But by October, another wave of the virus was washing over the nation, causing an obscene number of new cases and deaths.

As fall slipped into winter, the pandemic grew even more intense. The numbers—new cases, hospitalizations, deaths—climbed to new heights, eclipsing the obscene numbers we had seen in the spring. It was hard not to worry that that the virus was hopelessly out of control, with no relief in sight.

But as 2020 ended and 2021 began, there was a glimmer of hope: two vaccines received emergency FDA approval, and now the *real* fun began: figuring out how and where to get vaccinated. In the absence of a functioning federal government, it fell to states, localities and individual institutions to figure it out. Yes, those of us over 70 were to receive high priority, but for all practical purposes, chaos prevailed.

In my state, there were lists made available of pharmacies large and small, supermarkets, county offices, and other venues that were supposed to have vaccine available—except that they didn't. After a while, it seemed as though the only game in town was one large chain of hospitals, and the only way to access their vaccine was through its website. So after creating a user name and password, and entering all sorts of info, you could hit "SEARCH" and hope that an opening would pop up at one of their hospitals. No luck? Refresh! And refresh again! Perhaps nine times out of ten, there would be nothing available. But whenever you least expected it, the website would barf out a time slot at a random hospital. You would try to grab it, and after you entered still more information, you would learn that you were too slow, and the opening had vanished.

For me, this went on for the better part of two days. Maybe fifteen openings came and went, and I was never fast enough to nail one. Somewhere along the way, it got even tougher: they were now asking for your insurance information. (I suspect it had something to do with this: the vaccine itself was supposed to be free, but the hospital could ping your health insurance for administering it to you.) But near the end of the second day, I actually grabbed a slot! It was the very next day—no matter! And it was about 70 miles from my home—no big deal! Of course, this whole system was designed to deliver vaccinations to one individual, one at a time, so forget about getting vaccinated at the same time, in the same place, as your spouse. Still, by mid-February, my wife and I had received our two shots.

As 2021 progressed, large numbers of people were getting vaccinated. Which seemed really great, until some politicians decided that it would be bad for them if the new administration actually succeeded in getting the pandemic under control. Their efforts to dissuade people from being vaccinated, and trivialize social distancing, coupled with a highly contagious new variant of the virus, assured that the summer of 2021 was nearly as fraught as the summer of 2021 had been.

And in the fall of 2021, things went from bad to worse. A new variant—Omicron—proved to be insanely contagious, and the number of new cases exploded. The year 2022 began with new records being set every day. Then, as quickly as the new cases had spiked, they began to plummet. By February, people were—again—daring to suggest that the worst was over.

As late as Christmas 2021, we considered ourselves to be among the lucky ones who didn't get the virus, or if we did, it didn't affect us. But no one's luck holds out forever. Just before New Year's one of my daughters came down with Covid, with pretty bad symptoms, which was quickly followed by both of her daughters testing positive. And just after New Year's, her niece, my youngest grandchild, tested positive.

One couple among our friends were not so lucky. They both had it bad at the beginning in 2020, but thankfully they recovered. Not so fortunate was a college fraternity brother of mine. We had been close in college; but a tiff after graduation led to a half-century of no contact, which only ended at our 50-year reunion. When I learned of his death,

I was glad about our *rapprochement*; but felt stupid about how long it took.

Throughout the Covid-19 ordeal, people struggled to find some sort of precedent to what was happening. The terrorist attacks of September 11, 2001 were often mentioned, but the death toll that day—while horrific—didn't approach what Covid-19 did. I remember well how hesitant we all were to fly after the attacks, but that seemed to be the only scary threat hanging over us. That is . . . until just a week later, when another terrorist mailed letters laced with anthrax to five prominent people, and suddenly we were all afraid to open our mail.

Maybe a better precedent was the Cold War and particularly the Cuban missile crisis of 1962. The world's two superpowers appeared headed toward a war that could have gone nuclear in the ever so literal sense of the word. Or maybe the pandemic was akin to another phase of the Cold War: the Vietnam conflict that spilled over into Laos and Cambodia. The weekly casualty count scared the living daylights out of some of us who feared being drafted and who had drawn a losing ticket in the draft "lottery."

By sheer happenstance, during December 2020 and January 2021, I was listening to the audio book version of Erik Larson's outstanding work, *The Splendid and the Vile*" It tells the story—on a day-to-day basis—of Germany's relentless bombing of London and other cities in the United Kingdom in 1940 and 1941, during which some 45,000 Brits perished and many thousands more were critically injured. The damage to buildings large and small was incalculable. There was a constant fear that after all that death and destruction, the Germans would then invade and occupy the British Isles. But the British people dug in, pulled together, built hundreds of their own bombers and fighter planes week after week, and gave the Germans as good as they got, even taking the offensive and bombing German cities.

Of course, any comparison between the Blitz in Great Britain and the coronavirus in the United States is imperfect to say the least. For one, the U.S. had more than ten times as many deaths. And while dying from bombs exploding is frightful, the slower progression from Covid symptoms to hospitalization to a ventilator to morgue seems like purgatory itself.

And then there is this:

The British had Winston Churchill to lead the country through its ordeal.

We in the U.S. in 2020 had Donald J. Trump.

While these events made nearly everyone fear for their health and safety, the economic fallout from the Covid-19 pandemic was a whole 'nother story. A confession: a part of me had been rooting for a recession in 2020. I felt that the safety and stability of the United States—if not the world—depended on the incumbent president being defeated in November 2020. He had managed to skate past every scandal and outrage. He had taken credit for a thriving economy, so perhaps an economic downturn would take the wind out of his sails.

But 2020 was no mere recession. Job losses in the millions. Thousands of small businesses shuttered, many of which would never reopen. Government assistance botched and inadequate. Thousands of sick people with little or no health care and no financial cushion to pay for it. By the end of April 2020, I was waiting to see who would be the first to call this a depression. By June, the unemployment rate, which had hit an historic low just months earlier, had skyrocketed. Be careful what you wish for, I guess.

I suppose it was fortunate that the Covid pandemic occurred at a time that technology provided numerous channels allowing us to see and hear our loved ones: FaceTime, Zoom, and more. But one couldn't help wondering when we might be able to hug our kids and grandkids. The last thing I'd ever want to do was place them in jeopardy; but it seemed that the biggest impediment was putting us high-risk seniors at risk. Go figure.

So no, there really doesn't seem to be a precedent for the Covid-19 pandemic in the lifetimes of those of us in our 70s. It may yet turn out to be the most terribly strange *and* the most strangely terrible event of our lives.

CHAPTER 12

THE VERY STRANGE EXCELLENCE OF MEDICARE

Who could have imagined this?

Not I.

Who would have thought that after decades of being tortured by private medical insurers, in our old age, we would find ourselves in the Promised Land of predictable, hassle-free coverage—*Medicare!*

For umpteen years and decades while we were in the work force, my wife and I were covered by private insurance through our jobs. We were making a living, and a sizable chunk of that got deducted from our paychecks for our medical insurance. You would think we were "covered" in the event of medical expenses small (maybe?) and large (for sure), right?

We were fortunate that we never had to deal with catastrophic *medical* problems. But that doesn't mean we had no medical *insurance* problems.

Let's start with the process of just getting insured. There were any number of problems people like us faced regarding the selection of medical insurance. Which plan had the widest coverage? Which plan made the most economic sense? For a married couple who were offered very different coverages from their very different respective jobs, which would cover both of us best? Or should we each take what our own employers offered for ourselves?

Once all that was set, what about claims? No insurance company ever wants to pay *any* claim at *any* time. Period; full stop. Medical insurers are no different. I recall an incident when my daughter had surgery, a claim was filed with my insurer which was supposed to cover her, and it was rejected. I sought help from the lady at the surgical group who was their point person for dealing with insurance companies. When I expressed my exasperation to her, she chuckled, and explained to me that medical insurers *never* pay a claim the first time it is filed. They make you work for it, hoping that some people will just give up.

Who can forget those glory days of figuring which doctors were in the your "network." There was always at least one outlier or holdout, who—like Groucho Marx—wouldn't want to belong to any network that would have her. (Actually, she wouldn't join the network because it valued her time at less than the minimum wage.) And then there was the need to navigate copays, especially those that had to be paid up front before they let you see the doctors. (Ever have a situation where the doctor got paid *twice*? If so, has anyone ever gotten back any overpayment? This is a trick question. See Chapter 28 for the answer.)

Perhaps my worst memory of those days on private insurance was the dreaded arrival of an "EOB"—Explanation of Benefits. More often than not, these mailings advised you that there would be *no* benefits paid, and the "explanation" was the full equivalent of *no explanation at all.*

Just for fun, I dug into an old file of medical records to refresh my memory about those heady days on private insurance. I pulled out one entry to bring me back into the world of "Message Codes"—the footnotes that purported to be the "explanation" in my EOB. Are you ready?

> **Z036** THIS CLAIM HAS NOT BEEN SENT TO YOUR HEALTH REIMBURSEMENT ACCOUNT (HRA). *[Whatever that is, I never had one.]* OUR RECORDS INDICATE YOU HAVE OTHER INSURANCE. *[Nope.]* ONCE THIS CLAIM HAS BEEN PROCESSED BY THE OTHER INSURERS, ANY REMAINING BALANCE CAN

BE SUBMITTED TO THE CDH DEDICATED SERVICE UNIT. . . .

Z522 THIS SERVICE IS PAID UNDER THE PROVIDER'S CONTRACT WITH. . . . *[Paid by whom? Not you.]*

Z028 IF YOU ARE COVERED BY MORE THAN ONE HEALTH PLAN, YOU OR YOUR PROVIDER SHOULD FILE ALL YOUR CLAIMS WITH EACH PLAN. YOU SHOULD ALSO GIVE EACH PLAN INFORMATION REGARDING THE OTHER PLANS UNDER WHICH YOU ARE COVERED.

Z084c YOUR TOTAL COST SHARE FOR THIS CLAIM IS $23.04. *[What is the "cost share paid by the insurance company? Stay tuned.]* THIS INCLUDES ANY DEDUCTIBLES, COINSURANCE, COPAYS AND ANY OTHER AMOUNTS NOT COVERED BY YOUR HEALTH PLAN, INCLUDING ANY AMOUNT PAID BY ANOTHER CARRIER.

Y775b YOUR TOTAL COST SHARE FOR THIS CLAIM IS $23.04. THIS INCLUDES ANY

DEDUCTIBLES, COINSURANCE, COPAYS AND ANY OTHER AMOUNTS NOT COVERED BY YOUR HEALTH PLAN. [THE PROVIDER] WILL BE RESPONSIBLE FOR BILLING YOU FOR YOUR COST SHARE. *[They did indeed.]*

Y028c YOU HAVE MET $541.28 OF YOUR INDIVIDUAL DEDUCTIBLE FOR 2016.

Y029c YOU HAVE MET $541.28 OF YOUR FAMILY DEDUCTIBLE FOR 2016.

Y055c YOU HAVE MET $541.28 OF YOUR NETWORK COMBINED INDIVIDUAL DEDUCTIBLE AND OUT OF POCKET MAXIMUM FOR 2016.

Y056c YOU HAVE MET $541.28 OF YOUR OUT-OF-NETWORK COMBINED INDIVIDUAL DEDUCTIBLE AND OUT OF POCKET MAXIMUM FOR 2016.

Y105c YOU HAVE MET $541.28 OF YOUR NETWORK COMBINED FAMILY DEDUCTIBLE AND OUT OF POCKET MAXIMUM FOR 2016.

Y106c YOU HAVE MET $541.28 OF YOUR OUT-OF-NETWORK COMBINED FAMILY DEDUCTIBLE AND OUT OF POCKET MAXIMUM FOR 2016.

You may be wondering what medical miracle created the necessity for all these footnotes. Are you ready? Back in 2016, I was diagnosed with sleep apnea, and I had to sleep with a CPAP device. This was just one month's rent on the darned thing.

And I guess I should have given you a spoiler alert about this: how much was the charge that spawned all these footnotes? The giveaway was footnote **Y775b**, the one that said my "cost share" was $23.04. Guess I'm not very good at sharing, because $23.04 was the total cost.

There came a time when premiums for private health insurance skyrocketed to the point where they were taking huger bites out of paychecks every pay period. So the darlings at the health insurance companies came up with new "High Deductible" plans. How high was "High"? Well, you could go for most if not all of a year where they would make *no payment at all* until your expenses reached catastrophic levels. Of course, after a while, they jacked up the premiums of these High Deductible plans. But at least life was simple: you paid them massive amounts every month; you paid all the doctors; and the insurance companies paid out nothing—if you were lucky enough to have made it through the year with no major surgeries or other procedures.

In case you're wondering, I haven't forgotten that this book is about the strangeness of turning 70. And yes, Medicare becomes available at age 65. I waited until my wife was also 65 when we could both go on Medicare, so I was admittedly late to the party.

But boy, was the wait well worth it.

Imagine going to a doctor without first researching his or her "network" status. Just show up. No one asks for an on-the-spot copay. Weeks later, you get an EOB, but now there are really benefits to explain. Whatever the doctor might be inclined to charge for your visit, Medicare has declared that some smaller amount is fair and appropriate, and simply pays 75% of that figure. If you have a Medicare "Supplement," it pays the other 25%--no questions asked. There's one modest annual deductible, which means that you'll get a bill from the first doctor or two you see each year, so you have to pay them, but only the smaller fee negotiated by Medicare.

There is one complication, though, when it comes to prescription drugs, known as Medicare Part D. For that, you need to hook up with—gulp!—a private insurer, for which you have to pay a monthly premium. But I routinely find that my copay is zero on a number of prescription drugs I take.

All of this is strange enough to include in a book about strange things encountered after the age of 70. But there's more. After five years on Medicare, I can say that the system seems to work pretty darned well.

Which is stranger still, given that it's run by the federal government. (That's not so true with Part D. Because it involves private insurers, I've had some spectacular screw-ups in getting enrolled and arranging payment.)

During the 2020 presidential primaries, there was much talk of "Medicare for All," not just those over 65. I have no interest in getting into the politics of this issue, but I do think there are some misconceptions among people who oppose expanding Medicare. For one, no one is forced to go on Medicare at any age. For another it's not just a giveaway. Those with substantial incomes have to pay surcharges, which come out of Social Security payments.

But I would never give up my Medicare. At a time when many have to worry about new medical problems and worsening old ones, it is strange indeed to no longer have the added worry of taking a shellacking from a private health insurer, or death by a thousand footnotes.

CHAPTER 13

THAT STRANGELY TOXIC 2020 TAX ON 1975 INCOME

I can still remember it.

It was 1975, and the U.S. Congress had enacted legislation that created the new financial instrument known as the Individual Retirement Account, or IRA. It came at a time when fewer and fewer jobs—especially those in the private sector—featured old-fashioned pensions. It was a way to build a nest egg for retirement above and beyond Social Security.

Of course who in their 20s even knew anything about Social Security? And why should we, really? All we needed to know at the time was that it was a decidedly involuntary tax that took a substantial chunk out of your paycheck, above and beyond withholdings for federal and state income tax. Where that money went was anyone's guess.

But now we had a totally voluntary creature to consider—the IRA.

How did it work? It was quite simple. You could open an account with a bank or a mutual fund company and deposit up to $1500 of your annual income. And why would anyone do that? Because you would not have to pay income tax on those $1500. Yes, presumably, there would come a time when you would have to pay tax on that money—maybe if and when you make it to your 70s. But that would be multiple decades away. And by then, your income might have dropped and you'd be taxed, supposedly, at a lower rate.

What sold me on IRAs was this argument: if you *didn't* put that $1500 into an IRA, you would have to pay tax on that money at the end of the year. If your tax bracket was, say, 25%, that would come to $375. *And once you pay that tax, that money is gone forever.* Instead, with all $1500 in an IRA, all of it could be earning more money for you—for decades.

What a deal! As close to a no-lose proposition as you can get! So I dutifully kept making contributions for years. Then, at some point, employers began to offer the eponymous "401(k)" plan. (I often wondered what ever became of 401(a) through (j), though I didn't lose much sleep over it.) The broad concept was the same. You could channel some of your income into the plan, and in many instances, employers kicked in an additional contribution. And none of that money was subject to current taxation. The sizes of permissible contributions increased over the years, and—lo and behold—the nest egg grew.

While it may at first seem off topic, I should interject here that I have never owned a pet. I do like animals, and I have often enjoyed playing with (someone else's) dog or chatting with (someone else's) parrot. And because I never actually owned an animal, I never had the need to provide accommodations for them.

I mention this now only because shortly after I turned 70, a flock of chickens I had never met came home to roost in chicken coops I had never erected.

Yes, we are talking about an especially noxious creature known as the Required Minimum Distribution, or RMD. It is the government calling to remind us about that little detail we pooh-poohed back in the 1970s. You know, the one that said you will have to pay tax on that money when you get old—which they told us at a time when the very notion of getting old was incomprehensible.

What the RMD does is this. Starting when you turn 70 and a half, each year you are required to withdraw a chunk of that IRA account and pay income tax on it. They calculate these amounts based on your steadily declining life expectancy (what a happy thought!), so your account is emptied out by the time the government expects you to be pushing up daisies. And you are not just required to pay taxes on the amounts you contributed, like that original $1500. You also have to pay tax on the funds that were earned by your IRA contributions over all those decades.

And what is one supposed to do with the RMD you take out of your IRA or 401(k) account? Whatever you want. You can spend it. Or you can reinvest it in a nonpension account. But make sure you put aside a portion of it to pay the taxes.

So what is so toxic about this? I happen to think we shouldn't be punished for doing the right thing to keep ourselves from becoming homeless and dependent in our old age. And wouldn't it be better to keep all of those funds invested? If your IRA is with a bank, keeping the money there allows the bank to make loans for mortgages and whatever. Yes, you can put your RMD back into an account at the same bank, but if you've put aside money to pay the taxes, it won't be as much. In my opinion, for each year we *don't* take funds out of our pension accounts, we should be rewarded by having some portion of the account declared *nontaxable.*

Yes, I know this is the deal we agreed to back in the 1970s. And I will not pretend that I didn't know what would happen when I got old—I pretty much did. (An occasional warning, maybe every five or ten years, might have softened the blow.)

But I don't have to like it. And I don't.

CHAPTER 14

A STRANGE LOOK BACK AT THE FUTURE

Do you remember the future?

Do you recall being young and thinking about that highly theoretical and speculative concept known as the future? My guess would be this: hardly ever.

The lines of demarcation seemed clear 50 or 60 years ago. We lived in the present—both literally and figuratively. We were too young to have much of a past and, to us adolescents, there didn't seem to be much for us to say about our childhood.

But then there was the future. To the extent we ever gave the future a moment's thought as kids, the future was more or less synonymous with "growing up." A seemingly endless and vaguely defined notion called Adulthood: jobs; relationships; perhaps marriage; and maybe children. New pleasures, but also new responsibilities. Complexity piled on top of complication.

It seemed to us back then that the future could extend out for decades, maybe even the better part of a century. It had an approximate start time: maybe a decade away, maybe less. It had no clear sell-by date, beyond that ultimate abstraction known as death.

The future was something you could plan for. And according to some, it was important to do so; but most of us did not. At a minimum, the future was something one should not jeopardize by flunking out of school, getting arrested, conceiving a child out of wedlock, or the like. Of course, we would learn much later that life was what happened while you were planning something else. Back then, however, who knew?

Way back then, talk of the future often centered on technology that might get invented years or decades later. Detective Dick Tracy had a two-way wrist radio with which he could speak with his colleagues. Really? Perhaps food could be cooked instantaneously with invisible rays. Cameras without film? Anything seemed possible in the future.

So what strange things happened to the future when you turn 70? Are you ready for this? Drum roll please.

Well, for starters, our future is something of which there is now a whole lot less.

The specific life expectancy figures may change from time to time. But this much we know. Not everyone who turns 70 is going to be around to turn 80. And this news just in: if we make it to 80, our 70s will have been the shortest decade ever. If you think your 60s went by in a flash, better fasten your seat belts.

Still, what can our future hold, abbreviated though it may be? For ourselves, it could be a mixed bag. Good health—if we are fortunate enough to have it when we turn 70—is not going to last forever. The freedom/boredom of retirement? If we are still working, we may continue to have the satisfactions and aggravations of work. But if we haven't set the world on fire by now, it's probably not going to happen.

Are there still new inventions we can daydream about looming in the future? Some say everything that's important has already been invented. They're wrong, but this much is true: if we live to see them, there's a good chance we will be part of the pathetic group that can't figure out how to use them.

And then there is the future of our children and grandchildren—that is, *their* future as viewed through *our* 70-plus year old spectacles. Our children may be approaching middle age or may be there already. But by now, they have pretty much become the done deal they were destined to be. They may have more mountains to climb, and they may or may not get there. But if they do, we may or may not get to see it.

Of course, this reality is magnified with our grandchildren. Their future seems as unlimited as ours did 50 years ago. But we now find ourselves doing a lot of math. My grandkids will start college in, say, seven years. Will I get to see it? How about graduation? Marriage? The ultimate jackpot: great-grandchildren? Could I possibly make it to ninety?

Perhaps the one thing about the future we can know with certainly at this point in our lives is this. Any future we still have now will eventually become the latest chapter of our past. Next year will become source material for nostalgia the year after. We should still treat the future as a time to create memories.

CHAPTER 15

THAT STRANGELY ELUSIVE LUXURY KNOWN AS SLEEP

To sleep. Perchance to dream.

Or not.

To be clear, I am not suggesting that if one sleeps, he or she will not dream. To the contrary, if and when one does sleep, there is always a chance that dreams may come one's way.

No, my doubt is far more fundamental. For decades, I wondered if I would ever again get my fair share of sleep. When I turned 70, sleep became even more and more elusive to me. And this happened at a stage of life when my free time was at an all-time high, making my inability to fall asleep and stay asleep terribly strange and all the more frustrating.

It was not always so.

As an adolescent, I suppose I slept as much as the next person.

Which is to say I went to bed late, woke up later, and probably logged a good seven or so hours per night.

When I went away to college, I quickly learned that there were a few keys to how freshmen were expected to live at my school. First, go out drinking every night, even—indeed, especially—on "school nights." Second, come back to the dorm as late and as inebriated as possible. Third, if you have an 8:00 class the next morning, cut it. And fourth, if you could not cut the class, at the very least, you should sleep through it.

I was never much of a drinker, at college or even later, and I wasn't yet 18 years old during my freshman year. As for cutting classes, well, I shied away from it. No, I hadn't yet had the epiphany that my parents were shelling out hard cash for every one of those 8:00 classes. And I will not try to convince you that I tried to go to each class as a matter of learning for learning's sake. If I am being honest, I actually believed I might pick up some factoid at any given class that might turn up on an exam.

So, for the most part, I soldiered my way to each class, dragging not only my butt but also a serious sleep deficit. My college was up north, where it was anywhere from cold to freezing for most of the academic year. But the classrooms were warm and toasty. I would have to take off my winter coat, but if I folded it up in a certain way, it made a pretty decent pillow. About 10 minutes into each class, I was in dreamland.

Sooner or later, I had fallen asleep in every classroom on my freshman schedule. Math? Check. English? Sure. But my most fateful sleeping accomplishment occurred in a chemistry lecture in a massive auditorium. My napping through that snoozer should have been a real nonevent. And it was, until a few days later.

That is when my college's weekly student newspaper came out. That week, it had a big article about freshman chemistry. And front and center was a photograph of a student in that massive auditorium with his head down, buried in his coat. You could not see the poor wretch's face. But I didn't need to. I recognized my friend seated to my right, who was paying rapt attention to the proceedings. And when I looked a bit closer at sleeping beauty, while my face wasn't visible, I could indeed recognize my own shirt.

And this raised a potential problem. You see, my parents had taken a subscription to the college paper to have some idea what their noncommunicative son was up to. I'll never know if my observant and perceptive mom recognized the shirt and realized that was me. What I do know is that very soon after I made this splash, my parents received a poison pen letter from the dean of my college, alerting them to the fact that their pride and joy was in the process of flunking chemistry. It seems that all that sleeping had coincided with me bombing a major chemistry exam. Go figure.

Still, in the juvenile culture in which I was then wallowing, I had earned some bragging rights. Slept through at least one class in every subject! How cool is that?

Actually, not quite. There was one more mountain to climb.

At that time, freshmen at my school were required to take "physical education"—that is, gym—each semester. You had to rotate every few weeks from one sport to another, such as basketball, swimming, and so forth. Since I attended a college where hockey was a big deal, ice skating was another option. But for those of us of the nonathletic persuasion, the real prize assignment was bowling.

Now, this was the 1960s, and back home, I had spent as much time as the next guy at local bowling alleys. These were modern set-ups, with automatic pin setters and ball returns. But upstate at my college, things were a bit different. The gym was named after the Class of '87, and you will appreciate that this was not a reference to *1987*.

This gym was ancient. And so were the bowling lanes down in the bowels of the gym. They actually had *manual* pin setters! The ten pins had holes bored in their bottoms, and to reset the pins, you would have to step on a pedal at the far end of the lane, which pushed up ten prongs on which the pins would be placed, at which point the prongs could be lowered back below the surface. You will appreciate that this required the presence of a warm body.

Thus, when it was time to rotate from basketball or swimming to bowling, three kids were assigned to each lane. One, of course, did the actual bowling, and another was down at the far end setting the pins. That left a third guy whose job it was to keep score. He would sit on a bench behind a table upon which rested the scoring sheet and a pencil. By now, dear reader, you must have figured out *what else* was rested on that table.

I recall little about my relationship with sleep in the years immediately after college. There was graduate school, marriage, and the start of what would turn out to be a long career. But then, in my early 30s, I became a father. It goes without saying that having a newborn in your life can result in a loss of sleep. Babies wake up often during the night, and smaller babies have smaller stomachs that need replenishment more often. In one of the great blessings of my life, we had twins. Each of these little ones woke up several times most nights, and they didn't exactly try to coordinate these events.

Years later, younger colleagues who were expecting twins would ask me if it's tough to sleep with twins. My answer, which wasn't entirely tongue-in-cheek, was that it's only tough for the first 20 years.

By the time the 2000s rolled around, my sleep issues had become chronic. Pharmaceutical solutions offered occasional relief. By then, I had banished caffeine from my diet, and I even swore off chocolate after 6 p.m. in the belief that it was messing up my sleep.

In my late 60s, I graduated to the major leagues of sleeplessness. One of my doctors suggested that I take a "sleep test." I did take it. And

I flunked. I was now the proud owner of a case of sleep apnea, and my stable of doctors now included a sleep specialist. I came to learn that, without treatment, my breathing was stopping *hundreds* of times every night! Yikes. Why go to bed at all?

After a few years of breathing machines and dental devices—which may have kept me breathing but caused me to dread the mere prospect of going to bed—I was fortunate enough to shake my sleep apnea. I took another sleep test, and I passed. My sleep future looked bright.

That is, until I turned 70.

As I have shared, a couple of years into my 70s, I was forced into semiretirement, as a result of which instead of working maybe five or six hours a day, I was tending to work more like two or three hours a day. Then, in 2020, the Covid pandemic forced me into working from home or—more accurately—*not* working from home. And instead of spending two or more hours a day commuting, that added to my free time.

So, strangely enough, at a time in my life that I could easily have spared eight or nine hours a night sleeping, I seldom could sleep more than about six. I didn't seem to have much trouble *falling* asleep. My real problem was *staying* asleep. It might be 4:00 in the morning, but I would often wake up to visit the bathroom and I was absolutely, irretrievably, and emphatically awake. No amount of tossing or turning would allow me to go back to sleep. I was up for the day—but my day rarely lasted beyond 10:00 p.m., because by then I'd have been up for 18 hours!

By around the ninth month of the 2020 Covid pandemic, a strange thing started to happen. For no apparent reason I started to occasionally get seven hours of sleep, or even more. Then—and again for no apparent reason—after a day or two of this abnormal behavior, I'd revert to form, awakening at 4:30 a.m. without the slightest inclination to take another dive under the covers.

Of course, this book is about strangeness, and my sleep history took an unexpected turn around the time I turned 74. I was seeing a medical professional about another issue, and she felt the need to dig into my sleep issues as well. She had me go off my existing sleep medication and try something else that wasn't well known as a sleep aid. I was instructed to take one dose at bedtime and another if I were to wake up in the wee hours. Omigosh! It really worked. I started to regularly get seven or even eight hours, often sleeping straight through the night. When I did wake up at two or three A.M., I would take that second dose and it often got me back to sleep.

I've lived long enough to know that things which get better can also get worse. If I revert to sleepless nights, rather than fight it, I plan to plow ahead and figure out what to do with all the hours I am not sleeping. Maybe I'll realize my decades-long James Bond fantasy and become a spy.

But I can assure you of this: I won't be assigned to a sleeper cell.

CHAPTER 16

THE STRANGE LUXURY OF UNLIMITED INFORMATION

Back in the 1950s and 60s, when I had to do research for a project or a report for school, I was told to go to "the library." For me, that meant a local "branch" library in the Bronx. To access it, I would walk down a major street in my neighborhood, East Kingsbridge Road, to an unobtrusive little downhill street that was only for pedestrians, known as Coles Lane. At the bottom of that street sat the library, home to what I understood to be pretty much all the information that anyone might find useful. While you could borrow many books at the library, as I recall, you could not borrow "reference" books, since they had to always remain available to all comers.

Of course, the fact that this was a "branch" library drove home the fact that this was not the mothership of information. That, of course, was in Manhattan. For years, I thought that was the massive edifice in Bryant Park off Forty Second Street with the lions out front. I came to learn that was not the library from which local branches emanated. Still, it was a true wonder of the world. It seemed to house not only all the information you might need, but all the information *anyone* and *everyone* might need, *ever*. It had a staff that could look up and answer almost any question you might throw at them, even over the phone, and another staff that would track down and fetch any book under their roof—which was to say pretty much any book of any consequence.

Around the same time, an idea took hold that perhaps you didn't need to venture out to a small library or even a large one to do research. For a price, your family could have a reasonable facsimile of a library right in your rent-controlled apartment. Yes, this was the heyday of encyclopedias, and they were selling like hotcakes.

Perhaps the most popular one was the *World Book*. It was readable and accessible, and it seemed to touch all the bases needed for reports and projects up through high school. But my father had a bit of a scholarly bent, so for him, only the *Encyclopaedia Britannica* would do. It was thorough, dense, and—well—*British*. We all knew how smart the British were, or so they seemed. Entries were written by scholars, and if we mere mortals got to read their stuff, something was bound to rub off. Even their spelling of "encyclop**a**edia" was pretentious.

The folks at Britannica weren't just scholarly. They were good businesspeople too. After the salesman got you to sign up for the

24-volume set, he would point out that new knowledge was emerging every year, and in order to stay current, you should subscribe to their annual supplement, called something like "*The Book of the Year 196_*." Eventually, those supplements came to occupy more space than I did.

Looking back over six or so decades, it is impossible to pinpoint when it became understood that all the information in the world could not possibly fit in one set of books, or one library (large or small), or even in all of the libraries taken together. It likewise seems impossible to say exactly when you could come across a question—any question—and know, with reasonable certainty, that you could get an answer with just a modest amount of effort. And it is only a little less impossible to determine when you could do all that without moving away from your computer screen.

For now, in my seventies, I don't waste my energy answering those questions. What I do know is this: I am spoiled rotten by the incredible access to information I have and the ability to answer questions large and small with a few taps on my iPad.

I start most days with a cup of coffee and the print edition of the *New York Times*. But that's not entirely accurate, because if I wake up before the usual 7:00 a.m. delivery time, I will start reading some of the *Times* on my iPad. Yes, I am aware that the electronic version is more up-to-the-minute since the print edition may have been put to bed many hours earlier. But that's not why I go to my iPad; it's simply a matter of catering to my impatience. Like other dinosaurs my age, I still like the print edition, in part for the puzzles (see chapter 7), and because I sometimes stumble upon quirky articles in the print edition that elude me in the electronic versions.

But whichever version I'm using, I'm constantly going off on tangents on my iPad. Take, for example, locations. As discussed in the next chapter, I have had a lifelong obsession with geography. When I read an article that refers to a city, country, river, desert, or mountain I'm not familiar with, I go to Google Maps to scope it out. I often feel I cannot fully grasp *what* might be going on unless I know *where* it is happening. Or maybe there will be mention of an individual whose name I recall but who I cannot quite picture. But of course, I can: a quick visit to Google Images leads me to perhaps hundreds of photos of people as they look now and as they looked years ago.

Even watching TV or a movie has become problematic if my iPad is not close by. My wife and I will often see a cast member that we just *know* we have seen in earlier performances. A quick look on *IMDB* gives us every cast member and everything else that actor has been in. Mystery resolved.

And I haven't even mentioned the information everyone needs, every day, in almost every job.

I have become all too familiar with the expression "TMI." It is often a response to people who share too many details that we don't need and don't really want. I'm sure I'm as guilty of oversharing as the next person.

But I will say this here and now. As someone now slogging through my 70s, with names, facts, figures, and so much more leaching out of my deteriorating grey matter, it is simply impossible to have access to too much information.

CHAPTER 17

MY STRANGELY CHANGING ATTITUDE TOWARD LONGITUDE AND LATITUDE

I never quite figured out how I became obsessed with maps. Clearly, I did — many decades ago. But now, in my 70s, not so much.

It might have started with the *Encyclopaedia Britannica* which my family acquired in the 1950s, as I discussed earlier. The basic set was 24 volumes, and as I recall, Volume 24 was a somewhat modest atlas. But one of the extras you could purchase was a much larger atlas that had its own special slot in the bookcase (itself another extra) that was offered with the basic set.

I know I spent many hours browsing through that big atlas, which had maps of Europe, Asia, Africa, South America, and of course North America. Perhaps because this edition of the *Britannica* was marketed in the United States, the atlas included more detailed maps of every state, and I enjoyed checking all of them out, even though I had never visited many of them (and still have not to this day).

But those were not the only maps in my life back then. All the major oil companies, including Texaco, Gulf, and what was then called Esso, gave away free maps at their gas stations. If you were buying gas in, say, Philadelphia, the gas station might have a little rack of free maps that would help to navigate your way to remote parts of Pennsylvania, as well as Maryland, Delaware (which was—and remains—too small for its own maps, so it shared a map with Maryland and sometimes Virginia), New Jersey, and beyond.

And there were other ways to obtain maps. Each state's tourism office offered a free map of that state, which you might pick up at one of those welcome centers just over the border when you crossed into that state. And if you were a member of the AAA (the Automobile Association of America), you were entitled to "free" maps from them as well. You were also entitled to request and receive a "Trip-Tik" for a trip you were planning, which the AAA would prepare for you on a custom basis. They consisted of thin strips of maps, each illustrating one stretch of a given highway, bound by a plastic spiral, that followed the major routes; when you got to the end of one strip, you would flip to the next. And on the back of each strip was information about lodging and points of interest along that particular stretch of highway.

In those days, it made good sense to keep a bunch of maps from the oil companies or the AAA in the glove box of your car. If you got lost, and the guy pumping gas was unable to give you directions, a map might get you back on track.

But for people who took maps seriously—and by this time that included me—you needed a good set of maps, and you needed to keep them *current*. Remember: those were the days when new roads, bridges, and tunnels were being built all over the country, all the time. I recall how a new map might show a new freeway in broken lines, meaning that it was still under construction. If you picked up a copy of the same map a year later, it might now be a solid line—a new road was open!

I imagine most of the maps distributed by the oil companies and the AAA were used simply to help people get from Point A to Point B. I, on the other hand, coveted maps because I just liked to pore over them. I liked to see where places were in relationship to other places, and what was in between. I liked knowing what was close and what was far—and *how* far. If I heard the name of a city or town or radio or TV that was not familiar, I needed to know where it was.

I also had to have a sense about the roads that could take you from one place to another. And by this point new roads were proliferating. The Interstate Highway system! Want to drive from New York to LA? Get on I-80 in Teaneck, NJ, and make a left in Oakland, CA. I was surely the only kid on my block that knew that major north/south interstates ended in 5, east/west interstates ended in 0, and something I had never heard of—beltways around cities—started with 4 or 6.

During those years, I lapped up geographic trivia like a thirsty puppy. That weird circular border between northern Delaware and southeastern Pennsylvania. The fact that Terminal A of Newark International Airport (as it was then known) was actually in Elizabeth, NJ. The fact that Washington, DC is further west of New York City than it is south. Atlanta is west of Cleveland. Cape May, NJ is south of Baltimore. When you cross the Ambassador Bridge from Windsor, Ontario to Detroit, Michigan, you go north, not south. You get the idea.

While I might pore over the main body of a roadmap, I also had a thing for the insets. Yes, those little chunks of real estate that might, for example, give you some extra detail for, say, a smallish city. Insets also compensated for the geometric inconvenience of places that "stick out" a bit too much. On maps of the United States, Hawaii is always an inset, since no one needs to see all that ocean between Hawaii and California. Similarly, on maps of New York state, the eastern end of Long Island is often an inset, which you need to shift over to on your trip to Montauk Point (closer to Boston than it is to New Jersey!)

When I was in my 20s, I took my map obsession to a new level. Remember those racks of maps at the gas stations? Some of them—Texaco comes to mind—also had postcards you could fill out to ask for help on an upcoming trip. If, say, you were driving to Chicago from

New York, they would send you maps of New Jersey, Pennsylvania, Ohio, Indiana, and Illinois. It didn't take me long to discover that I didn't need to pretend I was planning a trip; I could just ask for a few maps on their postcard. A week or so later, the maps would arrive, with a bonus: another empty postcard. If you repeated the process enough times, you could accumulate maps of every state; maps of every major city; and even maps of Canada and Mexico.

Which is what I did.

I suppose it was inevitable that when everything else in our lives migrated away from paper, so would maps. And they did. Even before I turned 70, every smartphone and tablet had a "Maps" app. And they were pretty darn good. Sure, you were limited to maybe one square foot on your iPad, in contrast to a paper map that covered your kitchen table, but you could adjust your electronic map to cover as much or as little as you like. Of course, no insets: if you want more detail, just zoom in.

And who needs those old Trip-Tiks from the AAA? Many cars come with a navigation or GPS system which gives you turn-by-turn instructions. And apps like Waze can optimize your travel by taking into account real time traffic information.

Yes, I'm glad to have these tools, and I use them with appreciation. What geography junkie wouldn't love the graphics that show you exactly what your upcoming exit looks like? But I fear the day when paper maps will no longer be available. The last time I checked, the AAA still offers them, but who can predict how long that will last? I still have most, if not all, of my full set of Texaco maps; and while I will never throw them out, I rarely browse through them.

So while I embrace much of modern technology, in this one area, for this one aging Baby Boomer, some of the thrill is strangely gone.

CHAPTER 18

MY STRANGE ON AGAIN, OFF AGAIN, RELATIONSHIP WITH TECHNOLOGY

For over 50 years, I have managed to consistently remain about two or three years behind the curve in adapting to new technology. I suppose there's nothing really strange about that. Not all of us can be part of the vanguard, acquiring the latest devices, performing the newest tricks, and then bragging about it. Besides, sticking to the middle (or even the back) of the pack usually means there are smarter people around who can help me along.

As I coasted through my 50s and 60s, however, technology seemed to be exploding in new directions as never before. Still, I was able to muddle through, catching up enough to remain somewhat relevant and avoid much of the tech shaming that savvy youngsters often visited on the rest of us.

After turning 70, though, I thought the jig was up. Too many new tech developments were blossoming all over, and I thought I could never keep up. And by that I mean that I felt that I couldn't get into this new stuff even after my customary two- or three-year time lag.

Strangely enough, though, I was wrong. But to give you a full sense of this, I need to go back — *way* back.

All of us who are now in our early 70s entered college when computers were first becoming a really big deal. But it was an even bigger deal for those who went to engineering schools, as I did. I would eventually come to understand that I was a misfit in the world of engineering. Was I the type of kid that could change the spark plugs on a car? Not on your life. Build a ham radio set from a kit? You must be kidding. I was, however, pretty good in math and science, and this was still the early post-Sputnik, race-to-space era, with science and math being a bit of a national obsession. So, lacking any better idea, I took a pass on a liberal education, which haunts me even now, and jumped into the world of fluid mechanics, thermodynamics, electrical circuit theory, and differential equations.

At my college, there were thousands of slide rules. But there was only one computer. But it was a doozy, occupying the entire basement of the math building. A massive IBM mainframe. It's been said that my mobile phone has more computing power than this monstrosity, but back then, it was state of the art.

So it came to pass that in the fall of 1966 I took a course in computer programming that allowed me to use it. To prepare a program, you had to sit at a keypunch machine and create a deck of cards. You would put your deck in the queue and wait a couple of days for the few minutes it would take for your program to run — or not run, if it had bugs that you would have to fix.

During my brief engineering career, I actually had an opportunity to put my "computing" skills to work. I worked for a spell at what was then called General Foods, which had a frozen foods division known as Bird's Eye, which sold a product known as Cool Whip. The product was sold in plastic bowls, and automatic machines filled the containers up to the top. But this resulted in a bit more product being added than the weight promised on the label. So, in an effort to give away less "free" Cool Whip, a project was initiated to create a slightly (but unnoticeably) smaller bowl. I won't bore you with the details (unless you are my children, for whom it is too late, or my grandchildren, who have something to look forward to), but I worked up a computer program to calculate the volume of different versions of the new bowl. I never knew if the final design grew out of my computer program, since I left the job before the project was completed — and, soon thereafter, left the engineering profession altogether.

I went to law school hoping to put plenty of distance between myself and technology. But that was not in the cards. With engineering degrees on my resume sticking out like a sore thumb, I found myself having to choose between patent law and unemployment. As it turned out, my 47+ year run as a patent lawyer was pretty interesting. As I came to learn, you didn't need to be a hardcore techie to do patent law; you just need to know more about the technology you were handling than judges and jurors.

Early in my legal career, the concept of "personal" computers became a thing. For a very long time, it passed me by. Ironically, my wife — who had no technical training at all — plunged into those waters headfirst, to the point that she could talk technology, while all I could do was wax eloquently about the good old days punching cards in the basement of the math building.

In the early 1980s, computers finally made their way into the consciousness of lawyers in a big way: computerized legal research offered by LEXIS and WESTLAW. In those early days, to access those services, you had to buy or rent a dedicated terminal, which was mostly a piece of furniture with keyboard and hidden innards that connected — somehow — to some big computer somewhere else. After a decent interval while other law firms took advantage of this quantum leap in research, my law firm and I dipped our toes into those waters too.

While all this was going on, my children quickly got to the point where they were more comfortable—actually, *much* more comfortable—with technology than I ever was. And my grandchildren will surpass me before they get to high school as sure as birds sing in the morning.

So where does this leave me as a dinosaur now over the age of 70? I have struggled to keep up, or—more accurately—stay only a little bit behind. What I find most strange, though, is that I have been able to add a few new tech tricks to my arsenal this late in the game. For example:

- **UBER and LYFT!** Starting around the time I turned 70, every six months or so, a situation would arise where I needed to hail a ride, and no taxis were available. Of course, by this point, it had been so long since I used them last that I had completely forgotten how to work these apps and needed to check with my kids.
- **ZOOM!** Systems like ZOOM and TEAMS rescued the business world when the COVID-19 pandemic of 2020-21 made in-person meetings impossible. With some difficulty, I was able to join ZOOM and TEAMS meetings when invited. Eventually, around the time I turned 73, I got to be the one setting them up and inviting others. Me! Go figure.
- **BLINK!** This is one of those home security systems that takes pictures of people around your house stealing packages. In my

suburban neighborhood, the pictures are mostly of deer eating our shrubs or trash. I will not pretend that I was able to install our system. But I have been able to troubleshoot it once or twice with tech support holding my hand over the phone.

- **REMOTE DICTATION!** You will have surmised by now that I was never the type of lawyer that could just type (or should I say "word process" or "keyboard") his own briefs. For decades, I drafted briefs by dictating them and having my assistant transcribe them. For the longest time this required a physical handoff of one or more little microcassettes. Of course, the pandemic made that impossible. But I came to learn that I could download an app, dictate my brief on my cell phone, hit "send," and have it magically appear on my assistant's computer.
- **PARKING!** You may recall from my chapter on grandchildren that before the pandemic, I would routinely visit one pair of my grandkids on the Upper East Side of Manhattan and then the other pair on the Upper West Side. Each of these stops required me to park my car for maybe an hour or so, and this often required feeding a meter. I came to learn, at the age of 71 or 72, that there's an app for that. You set it up with the make, model, and license plate number of your car. Then, when you park, you enter the zone number, decide how long you plan to park (up to two hours), and you're set. If you start with, say, one

hour, and you need another 15 minutes, you can add time (and pay for it) remotely. I have actually done this stuff. Me!

So I am here to tell you that we needn't be intimidated by new technology. Sure, it's easy to say we don't need any new-fangled apps, devices, or tricks, but if we ignore them, they won't go away. We'll hear about them from others and have to make excuses for why we haven't joined the party. Most importantly, we will miss out on stuff. (Would you rather go feed the parking meter when it's 18 degrees out?)

If you take nothing else from this discussion, let me at least share with you what has likely been my biggest epiphany about technology in recent memory. It probably hit me a bit before I turned 70, but it seems to be the key to so many tech issues:

When in doubt, reboot!

CHAPTER 19

THE STRANGELY CONTINUING SHAMING OF A COUCH POTATO

If anyone were to declare that there is anything remotely physically fit about yours truly, several people will be deserving of credit. Alas, I am not one of them. Thankfully, at key crossroads in my life, someone I love was able to shame me into getting off the couch. It even happed again after I turned 70.

I spent much of the first half of my life being overweight, and all of that first half — as well as all of this second half — being a lousy athlete. I was slow, I was weak, and I pretty much did nothing about either condition. As a city kid, the options for sports were a bit limited where I grew up, but even as to those few I was pretty helpless. For example, kids in my neighborhood played a lot of stickball with a broom handle and a pink "Spaldeen." Kids would compete to see how long they could hit the ball by counting sewers — that is, how many of the spaced out manholes could you drive the ball from "home plate." Two? Maybe three? I was kind of a zero-to-one sewer kid. Then there was punch ball, to be played when there was no stick around. I could throw the ball up in front of me, and I could swing my fist at it ferociously. I just couldn't quite make contact on a regular basis.

One year my father signed me up for Little League. Loved that uniform! Loved the concept of pretending to be the Yankees! Otherwise…hated the experience. I think the idea was to let the good players have at it for maybe five innings, while the leftovers like me had to get one turn at bat, one half inning in the field, and go home. My batting stats: no runs, no hits, no walks, and no runs batted in. Fielding: no assists, no put-outs, no errors — unless one of the serious players accidentally hit the ball to right field where I was safely ensconced.

For ten summers I went to camp in the Catskill Mountains. I have always told people how much I loved camp, and I really did. Which is pretty remarkable when you consider what an athletic meritocracy camp can be, and — for me — was. Every sport involved the two best players "choosing up sides." Suffice it to say, I was no one's first draft pick — or second, third, etc. You get the picture. And I most assuredly never got to be the guy that was doing the choosing.

And then there was Color War. Four solid days of athletic competition. Four solid days of fearing that I will blow my team's lead. Here are two athletic personal highlights that stick in my mind all these years later. First, the big softball game. There was a huge buzz about the fact that I — little old me — hit a triple! When the story spread around camp, people omitted a few details. First, no one was on base when I hit it. Second, no one drove me home, so my team didn't even score a run on account of my efforts. And third: the only reason it was a triple was that everyone knew that I was an anemic hitter, so that the outfielders were pulled in and stationed just a couple of steps beyond the infield. Almost anyone could have hit the ball over their heads, and that one time I did.

My second highlight was the big Colorwar swim meet. Now you need to understand that for many summers at camp, all I could do in a swimming pool was tread water and maybe the dog paddle. But over time I learned how to do the "crawl," the side stroke, and — surprisingly — the breast stroke. When Color War rolled around, nobody deluded themselves into thinking I could win any event. But every kid had to be entered in at least one, and my event was the two-lap breast stroke. When the gun went off, the five other real swimmers took off, and I never saw them again. So I just tooled along: arms together; then out in front; then in a wide arc back to my sides. As I made the turn for the second lap, suddenly there were coaches walking alongside me cheering me on, telling me to just take it slow and make it to the finish line. When I did, there was cheering. I came to learn that several of my competitors had been disqualified for not doing the breast stroke correctly. Which meant that I took third place!

Things were not much better in high school. Actually, they were even worse. Here was the deal at my high school. There were fun sports to play outside during "gym," such as baseball and basketball. But in order to go outside, you had to first show proficiency in the dreaded "apparatus room." This meant that you had to demonstrate basic skills on the horizontal bar, the parallel bars, the pommel horse, and the rope climb. Let's just say that these requirements weren't quite basic enough for me. I don't remember if I ever made it out of the apparatus room. In case you're wondering, my high school had real sports teams, and they were pretty good. My best friend was on the track team. And me? I covered the track team for the school newspaper.

So it will not surprise you that by the time I got to college, I was starting to gain weight. And I kept on gaining for most of my life. Fortunately, there were interruptions along the way. Perhaps once every decade, I would go on a serious diet and lose maybe 40 or more pounds. But over the following decade, I would put the weight back on. My doctor would come to famously remark that I was capable of tremendous acts of will power for tremendously short periods.

My first shaming came around my late 30s. Those were the days when everyone was jogging, or at least talking about jogging. One day, my wife went out with our neighbor — not to jog, but to walk! My immediate reaction was incredulity: what for? What's the point? Jogging is exercise, while walking is just, well, sightseeing. Of course, who the heck was I to criticize? *I* wasn't jogging. I wasn't even walking. I wasn't doing a blessed thing.

But eventually I realized that walking was a helluva lot better than nothing. And so I sheepishly joined my wife in what became some four decades of walking, at an average pace of three miles per hour. A typical walk was an hour; and on weekends, when we had more time, maybe an hour and a half.

It didn't take long for us to realize that we couldn't walk in bad weather, and then some winter months presented entire weeks of bad weather, or roads and sidewalks covered with snow and ice. So I got shamed into buying our first treadmill; and since I of course cheaped out, that quickly led to more serious treadmills. In time, our treadmill welcomed a sibling: our first elliptical.

By my early 60s, my routine was pretty well set. I was a morning person, and I liked to get an early start on work when I still did it full time. So I worked out after work and my long commute home, either an outdoor walk or 45 minutes on the treadmill or the elliptical (that being the exact number of minutes it takes to watch a network drama on TV while fast forwarding through the commercials). And I did this six times a week, giving myself a rest on Fridays.

By my late 60s, it was time for more shame, this time from my older brother. When it comes to fitness and athleticism, any similarity between me and my brother is purely, well, nonexistent. He was a varsity athlete in college, and in his 70s he was a serious gym rat, extolling the virtues of muscle over fat. He patiently explained to me that cardio was all well and good, but if I was planning on surviving old age, I needed some strength too. So at the age of around 68, I joined a gym, took some training sessions, and started to work out on a wide array of machines designed to instill pain in muscles I didn't know I had. And I did this around twice a week until the Covid pandemic forced the closing of all gyms around March of 2020.

And this leads me to my most recent shaming. First, you need to know that my wife has, for some time, worked out twice a day. Long story, but all you need to know is that she's been in great shape for ages. In any event, in the early days of the Covid pandemic, I found myself at home pretty much 24/7. The gym was out, my workload had dropped considerably, and my commute was nonexistent. And —let's face it —being at home ineluctably led to taking in more calories, so something had to give.

So I started to work out in the morning, thinking I would just get it over with and relax for the rest of the day. As it was now spring and the weather was getting pleasant, and having already worked out in the morning, we started to venture outside for a late afternoon or early evening walk. Yes, we were in Covid panic mode, but we quickly got accustomed to toggling from one side of the street to avoid other folks and wearing masks when we couldn't. This was fine when the weather cooperated. And when it didn't, well, we weren't about to take the evening off. We just descended to what we affectionately call the dungeon and climbed aboard the machines.

And so, at the age of 73, I found myself working out not once a day, but twice. And what about my days off on Friday? Forget it! With another dose of shame, my old routine of six workouts a week had now been ratcheted up to fourteen.

To tell the truth, I'm not really unhappy—just a bit exhausted. I guess the real regret is that some of this shaming didn't happen sooner. If it had, maybe I could have stretched that triple in softball into a home run. Or maybe I could have taken *second place* in the breast stroke. And maybe my record in Color War would have been better than three wins and seven losses.

CHAPTER 20

MY STRANGELY EVOLVING LOVE AFFAIR WITH BOOKS

You would think a guy who goes to the trouble and expense of writing and publishing a book — even through what used to be called a "vanity" press, a/k/a self-publishing — must really like books, or maybe even love them.

And you would be right. I do, and I have loved books ever since they stopped being force-fed into me, which is to say since I graduated high school. Not surprisingly, over the course of my lifetime, books have changed, and so has my relationship to books. But the strangest change of all has been taking place since I crossed the threshold into my 70s. We will get to that, but first some history.

Every one of us had to read books in high school (or even earlier), and either write "book reports" about them or be tested on what we have read. As it happened, I had the amazingly good fortune to have as my high school English teacher — for all three years — the same sophisticated and erudite gentleman, for whom "Great Expectations" represented not so much a reading assignment as a projection of how his students would perform. In my sophomore year, he had us read *A Tale of Two Cities*, a few chapters each week, with a series of short quizzes along the way. All of which I bombed completely. It seems I was reading the words, but not processing them. It managed to go right past me that Sydney Carton and Charles Darnay were lookalikes, which (I later came to learn) was pretty much a central plot point.

I think I started to read books for pleasure during Christmas break of my freshman year of college. To be sure, it had nothing to do with college *per se*. And nobody would call what I chose to read *literature.* For heaven's sake, I was an engineering major! Books?!?!?! Instead, it had everything to do with a movie: *Goldfinger.* This was the third James Bond movie — I had not yet seen the first two — and it blew me away. I wanted as much James Bond as I could get, but the first two movies were no longer in theaters, and it was still years before Blockbuster. But there were books — the same books by Ian Fleming on which these early Bond movies were based. And they were available, in paperback, for the princely sum of fifty cents. (Yes, paperback. In my world, in those days, the notion of buying a hardcover book was unthinkable, not unlike paying a toll when a parallel road could get you to the same place for free.)

Much to my surprise, these Bond books were as much fun as a movie. My most vivid recollection is a scene in *From Russia With Love*, in which Bond is captured by a Soviet agent who is sitting across from Bond on the Orient Express. (Where else?) The agent tells Bond that when they enter a tunnel in a few moments, there will be a lot of noise, which will muffle the sound of the agent shooting Bond through the heart. As the tunnel draws near, Bond nonchalantly puts down the hardcover book he is reading (no paperback for 007!), pulls out a metal cigarette case, and lights up one last smoke. He then places the metal cigarette case inside the book, closes the book, and as they enter the tunnel, he places it over his heart—where it stops the bullet. Fleming had me imagining the bullet burning the first half of the book, the cigarette case, and the second half of the book before burning a hole in Bond's shirt when it ran out of steam.

You couldn't make this stuff up! That is, unless you were Ian Fleming. I was hooked. I bought every Bond book I could find. They even distracted me from the main events of my second semester of college: fraternity rushing and pledging.

In the years and decades that followed, I became a pretty avid reader. Mostly fiction, some of it pretty lowbrow (think Clive Cussler); some a bit more grownup (think Philip Roth). Around my 50s, I started to enjoy biographies and other nonfiction (think David McCullough; Erik Larson). The maturity level of my reading started to approach where I should have been in my 30s, but I suppose better late than never. I would tend to read in spurts: not much for weeks at a time, then a sprint during vacations.

The single biggest change in my reading was the introduction of the Kindle e-reader. I could swear I have been using Kindles for 20 years or more, but they first came out in 2007, when I turned 60. While I was never one to lead the charge with new technology, I was an early convert to the Kindle. Yes, I missed the feel and the smell of books. And yes, I appreciate that real books do not have to be recharged. But I have stuck with my Kindles (now on my second, after my original one could no longer be updated), and I never looked back.

Here is one thing I love about my Kindle: the ability to search within a book. Often, as I slog through a long novel, I am prone to forget who certain characters are. With Kindle, I can plug the character's name into the search box and turn up the first and all subsequent references to that character, which will invariably refresh my recollection. And here is another: when I go on a long vacation trip (say a 10-day cruise bracketed by two long flights), I can sometimes read four or five books. A Kindle can hold hundreds of books; without it, I would need an extra suitcase. And one more thing: on your Kindle, you can buy old classics that are out of copyright for a song. (For example, you can purchase *A Tale of Two Cities* for about two bucks. Which I did a few years ago, and I *still* could not get through it!)

By now you may be wondering what happened between me and books after I turned 70. Like so many things, this occurred during the Covid pandemic of 2020-21. In the years before Kindle, I had accumulated a pretty large closet filled with books. I had read virtually all of them. The few that I had not read resulted from a game I played for several years with my brother, who was always a voracious reader. Each of us would occasionally patronize the "remainder" tables at bookstores, where hardcover books could be bought at a fraction of the list price. Sometimes they were good reads. Other times, the blurbs on the book jackets were the only things worth reading. So when my brother finished working through a half-dozen or so of these books, he would pass them along to me; and vice versa. It is a good bet that some of these books made round trips between his house and mine. Maybe even more than one.

In any event, during the pandemic I had sporadically tried to reduce some of the clutter in my home, and around the time we were approaching the 12-month mark of the pandemic, I turned my attention to my overflowing bookshelves. So, I embarked on a project to organize my books alphabetically by author and cull out those that I could not justify keeping any longer (which filled about a half dozen big trash bags).

Throwing out books was a line I was reluctant to cross. Books had been entertaining and educating me for over half a century. It seemed almost sinful. So before trying to offload them, I gave them one more look to see if I might still read them. Not the paperbacks: not only were they falling apart, but the print was so ridiculously small. (No such problem with a Kindle — adjustable fonts!) As for the hardcovers, I picked out a W.E.B. Griffin novel that I could barely lift. When I got into bed to start reading it, I had to rest it on my chest, causing the kind of pressure that you read about as a warning sign of cardiac distress.

So I proceeded with my plan to get rid of these books, and I knew this might be challenging. Many years earlier, I used to be able periodically to bring a box or two of books to my local library. They would sometimes absorb them into their collections, and what they did not wish to keep, they would sell at a fundraiser. But years later, they were no longer interested. At least once, during the early aughts, I deliberately (and anonymously) dropped off a box of books after the library was closed for the evening.

So, what was I to do with a few dozen books in 2021? Once I accepted the fact that I was actually going to get rid of books, the question became how to do so. I tried to put them out in a separate bin with my regular trash, and they were still where I left them after the pickup. I then tried to treat them as paper to be recycled, along with my dozens of Amazon cartons. No dice.

You are not going to like this, but here goes. In March of 2021, at the age of 73, this lover of books started to hide one or two old books in the middle of each bag of kitchen trash, somewhere between the cantaloupe skins, the tuna cans, and the coffee grounds.

Strange enough for you? Don't say I didn't warn you.

CHAPTER 21

THE STRANGELY MOVING GOAL POST OF "REAL MONEY"

Many people our age remember a colorful politician from our youth named Everett Dirksen. He was a U.S. Senator from Illinois and was Minority Leader from 1959 to 1969. Dirksen was a real old school orator, and he was known for his quotable quotes long before "sound bites" became a thing. For example, he was once quoted as saying, "I am a man of fixed and unbending principles, the first of which is to be flexible at all times."

But perhaps the most memorable quote attributed to Senator Dirksen was this one: "A billion here, a billion there, pretty soon, you're talking real money."

Before we get into the meaning of this statement, we need to pause and acknowledge this: it has never been conclusively documented that Dirksen really said it. According to wikiquote.org, Dirksen was once asked about it, and he responded, "Oh, I never said that. A newspaper fella misquoted me once, and I thought it sounded so good that I never bothered to deny it."

For our present purposes, let us put aside the genesis of this statement and recognize that it's the thought that counts, especially when the thing we're counting is money. And the little bit of strangeness that I would like to share with you here is this: in the 2020s in which we now find ourselves, we seem to have arrived at a point that a billion dollars is no longer "real money." In the waning days of the Trump Administration and the early days of the Biden presidency, in response to the Covid pandemic and the economic damage it had wrought, our government has been proposing, debating, and enacting measures involving *trillions* of dollars. And nobody seems to bat an eyelash at these figures.

Let us use the perspective that old age gives us to try to understand these figures. When we were kids, the notion that someone might have a million dollars in the bank was somewhere between abstract and unthinkable. When I graduated college in 1968, the starting salary for engineers was a bit over $9000 per year. By 1974, newly minted lawyers at major law firms were paid about $18,000. Sure, people earned more as they accumulated experience. But a million dollars? It was hard for us mere mortals to imagine.

Of course, we would occasionally read about millionaires in the newspapers. And, in time, we might hear about someone who was dubbed a *multimillionaire.* But this often referred to someone who was worth two or three million dollars.

I am not sure when we first began to hear about *billionaires,* though I'm pretty sure it was well after the Everett Dirksen era. Bill Gates is said to have become a billionaire in 1987 and Mark Zuckerberg in 2008. I suspect Michael Bloomberg was already a billionaire when he was first elected Mayor of New York City in 2001.

But it is easy to forget what a billion dollars is. If you are an "entry level" multimillionaire, you may have accumulated two or three million dollars. *But a billion is a thousand million.* It looks like this: $1,000,000,000.00. At some point in college math I learned about "imaginary numbers," the basic unit of which is the (unimaginable) square root of minus one. In every real sense, to most real people, a billion dollars is a truly imaginary number.

So now we aging Baby Boomers must come to grips with the concept of a *trillion* dollars. Once again, we need to understand that we are not just talking about a few billion dollars. In 2020, *Forbes* estimated that Donald Trump was worth $2.5 billion (technically a multibillionaire) and that the world's richest man, Jeff Bezos, was worth $113 billion. But this does not even approach a trillion dollars. *A trillion is a thousand billion, or — if you prefer — a million million.* It looks like this: $1,000,000,000,000.00. Talk about imaginary numbers.

According to a website on the internet, a trillion $1 bills, laid end to end, would measure 96,906,656 miles.

I suppose the snarky comment made (or not made) by Senator Dirksen about billions of dollars was intended to suggest that back in the 1960s, even a billion dollars did not by itself, meet the threshold of "real money." Perhaps when you are dealing with the money funneled to Washington by hundreds of millions of taxpayers to finance the nation's defense, entitlements, and countless other expenses could only be understood in terms of billions of dollars. But that was a half a century ago. Are we now at a point where we need to envision "a trillion here, a trillion there" in order to contemplate "real money"?

Yes, there is always inflation to consider. I spent much of my youth listening to my parents reminisce about how much cheaper things were back in the day. As discussed in a later chapter, I have spent years paying that form of torture forward to my own kids and grandkids. But let's get real. The first gallon of gas that I bought during the Dirksen era set me back around 30 cents. Today, it's about 15 times as much. The first new car I bought with my wife was a 1975 Toyota Corona which cost about $4000. A comparable car today is maybe seven times as much. So how is it that "real money" today is as much as a *thousand* times what it was in Everett Dirksen's 1960s?

If you're looking for an answer, don't look at me. I graduated from college with as little an understanding of economics as the American system of higher education allowed back in the 1960s, and it has been all downhill since then. My only mission here is to comment on things that are strange—or even terribly strange—to those of us in our 70s. A trillion dollars is no more strange to me than a billion dollars, because neither is comprehensible. To suggest that one needs to reach either level to constitute "real money" is itself strange—and strangely unreal.

CHAPTER 22

THE SUPPOSEDLY TERRIBLE PAST AND THE STRANGELY EXCELLENT REALITY OF TELEVISION

In 1961, there came a moment when the world of television stood still. It was all about a speech by a formerly obscure bureaucrat named Newton Minow. Minow was a lawyer from Illinois who had worked in the two unsuccessful presidential campaigns of Illinois Governor Adlai Stevenson. After John F. Kennedy took office as president, he appointed Minow to be the Chair of the Federal Communications Commission, the government agency that regulated the television industry.

It was 1961 and I was well on my way to a lifetime of watching what most would consider far too much television. I had begun life at around the time TV was first becoming popular. In those days, it was a big deal when a family got its first TV set. Back then, a TV set was a piece of furniture, with a little screen housed in a big wooden console. It had a wire snaking out the window, up to the roof, and attached to an antenna. When something went wrong—which was quite often—you would get a visit from the TV repairman. He would look through the back of the TV set, figure out which of many vacuum tubes was on the fritz, and replace it from the box of replacement tubes he carried.

This was well before *Sesame Street* and *Mister Rogers' Neighborhood*, so I was weaned on the likes of *Howdy Doody* and *Kukla, Fran and Ollie*. As I moved into adolescence, I would start to watch more adult fare, such as comedy and variety shows and the occasional drama, such as *Dragnet* and *Highway Patrol*—among the first of countless police procedurals I would consume in my lifetime. Of course, there was one constant back then: whatever you chose to watch, it was in black and white.

Just a few months into his role, Minow gave a speech at a convention held by the National Association of Broadcasters. Here is what he said to broadcasters about what they were broadcasting:

> [W]hen television is bad, nothing is worse. I invite each of you to sit down in front of your television set when your station goes on the air and stay there for a day without a book, without a magazine, without a newspaper, without a profit and loss sheet or a rating

> book to distract you. Keep your eyes glued to that set until the station signs off. I can assure you that what you will observe is a *vast wasteland.*

The hue and cry was immediate and it was deafening. *A vast wasteland!* Critics of TV had a field day and much of the press simply piled on. For decades, television operated under the immovable cloud of Minow's disparagement.

Other media seemed immune from Minow's tarring. Take newspapers, for example. Yes, there were quality broadsheets like the *New York Times* and the *Herald Tribune.* But there were plenty of tabloids which were as trashy then as they are now.

Or take the movie industry. Even then, it cranked out hundreds of new movies each year. Many were terrific, but plenty were destined to be "second features" or worse. Interestingly, TV stations have been broadcasting movies for as long as I can remember, going back to the *Million Dollar Movie* on a local New York station, WOR-TV Channel 9, starting in 1955. However, there came a time when the networks began to offer "made for TV" movies. For many, that label was the kiss of death. If it didn't come out of a big Hollywood studio, how good could it have been?

But as I think back over all these decades, I cannot help but think that even back in 1961, TV was getting a bad rap from Minow and his claque. In fact, as it turns out, Minow himself was more than a little ambivalent about TV. Until I started to write this piece, I had never seen or heard of the first sentence of Minow's famous speech. Right before saying that when TV is bad, nothing is worse, he said, "When television is good, nothing—not the theater, not the magazines or newspaper—nothing is better."

Strangely enough, he was right. And that first sentence of Minow's speech would be vindicated in spades as decades flew by, as those of us over 70 have witnessed.

When Minow gave his speech, there was already a great deal of fine programming on "network" TV—which was pretty much the only TV to be had at that time. It included shows such as *The Twilight Zone, Alfred Hitchcock Presents, Perry Mason, Maverick* and *The Untouchables.* A few years later, they were joined by one of my favorite shows ever: *The Fugitive,* starring David Janssen as Richard Kimble, a doctor wrongfully convicted of murdering his wife, and Barry Morse as Lieutenant Philip Gerard, a latter-day Javert who was—as we were reminded each week—obsessed with Kimble's capture.

There have always been excellent shows on TV since those early days. The 70s gave us *Columbo* and *M*A*S*H* among others. The 80s gave us great stuff like *Hill Street Blues* and *St. Elsewhere,* about which I have already effused in another chapter.

The advent of cable TV gave us a whole 'nother plethora of superb programming, both on "basic cable" (not to be confused with free cable, which doesn't exist) and "premium" cable. This has included, in no particular order, *The Wire, Homeland, Ray Donovan, Billions, Breaking Bad* and its "prequel" *Better Call Saul, Fargo* (which, in fairness, started out as a movie but—in my view—improved when it moved to the small screen), and—most recently—*Mare of Easttown.*

As good as all this was, it was all just a preview of the explosion of great content that accompanied the advent of streaming. While it's hard to recall all the great stuff I've seen on platforms like Amazon Prime, Hulu and Netflix, here are a few: *The Crown, The Marvelous Mrs. Maisel, Ozark, Broadchurch, The Queen's Gambit, The Man in the High Castle* and *Little Fires Everywhere.* And streaming has opened the door to huge amounts of great programming from all over the world. This has included shows from English speaking countries such as Australia and, of course, the United Kingdom, where the BBC's production of quality programming is positively prolific. But I also have seen excellent shows from countries like Mexico and Spain, where subtitles are always available and there is often first-rate dubbing. One of my surprise favorites was *Borgen,* a show made in Denmark about the Danish government. I never imagined how good this would be.

So where does this leave Newton Minow's "vast wasteland?"

If you are among the chosen few who decide which shows should receive Emmy nominations and awards, you would probably point the (middle) finger at good old network television. Among the nominees for the 2020 Emmy awards, the network shows were practically shut out. There was one network nominee out of eight for Outstanding Comedy Series, none out of eight for Outstanding Drama Series, and none out of five for Outstanding Limited Series.

Are we to believe that shows on network television just don't measure up? Are TV shows not worthy of recognition simply because they can be watched by mere mortals without a streaming subscription or even a cable connection?

I respectfully disagree. In my humble opinion, there is a lot of very good content on network TV, and some that is really excellent. Take, for example, *This Is Us*. It got a lot of play and plaudits its first season or two, after which it sank into that large bucket of shows that get ignored by the Emmy folks. But it continued to be outstanding, season after season, episode after episode, with new characters, new twists, and new story lines, right up to the series finale in the spring of 2022.

And you can scoff at this if you want, but I happen to think that most if not all of Dick Wolf's shows are tremendously entertaining. For over two decades, he has been coming up with new shows with great story lines. With his Chicago franchise—*Chicago Med, Chicago Fire* and *Chicago P.D.*—he moved the concept of "crossovers" between shows to a new level.

As the Covid pandemic of 2020-22 starts to wind down, after

watching what may add up to a thousand hours of television, to whatever extent I emerge with any remaining semblance of sanity, I will make this terribly strange statement only once:

Thank you, vast wasteland.

CHAPTER 23

THE STRANGE OVERLOAD OF TERRIBLY SAD NEWS

In the second week of May 2021, word arrived that someone I had known for many years, who I will call "J," had passed away after a long series of medical crises. I had met J in 1974 when I was about 27 years old. We later worked together for several years starting when I was about 34. We had been promoted at the same time. J later moved on; I did not. But we saw each other from time to time until we gradually lost contact. When I heard about J's passing, we had been out of touch for 10 years or so, but I was saddened to learn of his ordeal.

A few minutes after absorbing this news, I remembered that another contemporary I had known for decades had passed away about two weeks earlier. I had just received that other piece of sad news during the *first* week of May, and I had talked about his passing at lunch with a mutual friend.

So for about a minute or two after learning of J's passing, I sat there trying to answer this question:

Who was that other guy again?

Seriously?

Oh yes! He had been a classmate in graduate school, who I will call "M." We met in 1971 when I was about 24 and spent time together discussing class work, sharing meals, and so forth. After we graduated, M and I ended up living near each other for a few years, and we socialized occasionally with our wives. As with J, M and I kept in touch for a number of years—until we didn't.

To be sure, there is nothing at all strange about the increasing frequency of our contemporaries dying after we turn 70. We know that it is statistically inevitable. But what *is* strange is this: the fact that I could forget—even for just a moment—who it was that died just a week or two earlier.

People in our orbit have been dying for all of our six plus decades. It might have started with our grandparents and their generation. At some point, we came to learn—increasingly often—about deaths among the generation of our parents.

But for many decades, the death of one of our contemporaries remained a rarity. Sure, there were deaths when we were, say, in our 30s. But it was often a fluke: an accident; a rare disease; even suicide. But for most of our cohorts, we could take comfort in the statistical probability that we still had many years ahead of us.

But that changed for me some time in my 50s. In the space of about two years, I learned that *four* friends—all from different segments of my life—had passed away.

- There was my buddy from summer camp. We had formed a sort of non-jock posse from 1955 all the way to 1964 when we graduated from separate high schools. We had stayed in touch during college, but inevitably our contacts became few and far between. I learned of his passing in an obituary in the newspaper where he worked.
- Then there was a friend from high school. We had met in tenth grade and kept in touch, on and off, through and beyond college. In the early 90s he had been an associate dean who coaxed me into a teaching gig, which I came to enjoy immensely. He then landed a job as dean at a distant institution, but sadly died suddenly of a heart attack after just a few weeks in his new position.
- Another friend, who I met in 1961, was initially the crony of a cousin of mine. His college was a relatively short distance from mine, and he would sometimes drop by. During the years between college and grad school, and then thereafter, we hung

out with great regularity, and attended each other's weddings. His passing from a medical issue that deteriorated disastrously came out of the blue.

- Finally, there was a guy I worked with at my first job. He was a year or two senior to me, so he was not just a friend but a bit of a mentor. His New York based company had sent him to California to help open a West Coast office, and he died a short time after making the move.

I recall feeling a bit shell-shocked from all this. It was too much, too soon. But then things stabilized, and people started to again pass away at a more "on schedule" rate. People who were dying went back to being mostly older than me. And while there were still some contemporaries who did not make it to old age—at my 50-year high school reunion there was a surprisingly long list of classmates who had passed at one time or another—there wasn't another cluster of the type I experienced in my 50's.

Until 2021, that is.

I need to add here that in the *fourth* week of May 2021, after I had drafted this chapter, word arrived that *another* contemporary of mine, who I will call Z, had passed away. Z was a fraternity brother from my pledge class at college. Yes, another guy that was my age. As I sat there trying to process this latest news, I thought about the two other deaths

I'd learned about that same month. And I blanked again! Not about my old friend M; I now recalled his passing quite clearly. This time I blanked on J.

And it turned out that 2021 wasn't quite done with my contemporaries. Around the summer, I learned that another fraternity brother from my graduating class, who I'll call S—who I considered a good friend with whom I *had* stayed in touch all these years—had been diagnosed with a rare form of leukemia and was in treatment. As summer turned to fall, I learned that S had transitioned into palliative care, and then into hospice. The end came swiftly in October.

When I paused to review the tally, I had no trouble remembering J and M. But this time, Z took me a little while longer.

There is nothing really strange about the accelerated rate of our contemporaries passing away. It would be strange if that *did not* occur now that we are in our 70s. This would seem especially true during a pandemic, though none of J, M, Z and S died from Covid.

But to blank on an old friend's passing just a week or two later? Sure, we all have senior moments. I've been having them since middle age, forgetting names, dates, details and other trivia. So now I am wondering if nature is cutting this senior citizen a break: through a brief brain freeze, I was being spared—just for a moment—the extra sadness that one friend's passing adds to those of others that we have lost.

CHAPTER 24

THAT STRANGELY INEVITABLE LOSS OF ALTITUDE

It was just a fluke, really. A small, almost painless shock that came out of left field, or maybe out of nowhere. If any one of several small events had not happened, we wouldn't be having this discussion. But they did happen, and so here we are.

It was May of 2021, and it seemed (falsely, as it would turn out) to be the beginning of the end of the Covid pandemic. Like turtles poking their heads out of their shells to check things out, my wife and I were taking baby steps on the way back to normalcy. So it was, for the first time in 14 months, that we took an excursion to our favorite outlet center for a bit of shopping.

I didn't need very much. I rarely do. I am not a shopper, and in an earlier book, with just a wee bit of sarcasm, I claimed to be the kind of person who uses clothes until they turn into lint in the dryer.

To be sure, over the previous 14 months I had not worn out much of my wardrobe. But my last pair of sneakers were starting to give up the ghost and I needed a new pair. (Success.) Also, my sandals had seen better days—even before the pandemic, during which I wore them constantly during spring, summer and fall. (No luck.)

I also needed a pair of blue jeans. I had a pair of Levi's (505's if you're curious) that I had tortured for days, weeks and months on end, with occasional time off for the washing machine. A hole was starting to form near my right knee. And the bottoms of both legs had started to get ragged.

So I paid a visit to the Levi's outlet and quickly found the 505's. They were more or less sorted by waist size. There's no need for me to share my waist size with you; but I can assure you that no one has ever called me Slim. In any case, ever the optimist, I went straight to the same waist size as my old 505's. Although I hadn't gained any appreciable weight over the course of the pandemic, I was still a wee bit anxious about fitting into my old waist size.

But waist size only tells half the story. Off-the-rack pants also come with a length or inseam measurement. And for as long as I could remember, I wore a 30 inch length. Pants usually come in only even numbered lengths, and there may have been a time when having pants flop over your shoes was a thing, which may have prompted me to try 32's. But that had been decades ago.

So as I sifted through the 505's in my waist size, I couldn't seem to find a pair with a 30 inch length. I was about to explore other options when—lo and behold—I found a pair with a *29*-inch length. I hadn't even thought that this was a possibility. But I figured I would try them on and see what they looked like.

My first surprise was that my old waist size still fit. Yes! But then I put on my shoes and looked in the full-length mirror to get the whole picture.

I'm not sure what I was expecting. Would the bottoms reach only to the top of my socks? If I were to go without socks, would my unsightly ankles be on display?

Well, my second surprise was this: the 29-inch length was *perfect.* And when a salesperson then belatedly handed me a pair with a 30-inch length, and I tried them on, they were *just too long.*

As slow on the uptake as I am these days, it didn't take me long to process this information. My torso was now about an inch closer to *terra firma* than it used to be. There was no more avoiding it. No more uncertainty or ambiguity. *I was shrinking.* And then there was this epiphany: those ragged bottoms on my old jeans got that way because they were too long and I was stepping on them.

The men in my family have tended to be on the tall side. My father was close to six feet tall, and my older brother topped out at over six feet.

I came close to six feet—maybe five feet eleven inches—but I never actually broke six feet. I suppose on some level this had been a disappointment. Still, most people tended to describe me as tall, and I'd be lying if I denied that this was a part of my identity. But if I could have traded an inch or two of height for a narrower waistline, I'd have made that deal.

I guess it would be a cliché (or worse) to say that getting shorter is just one part of the overall loss of stature we suffer as we age, especially for those of us of the male persuasion. Like most cliches, it's pretty much true. When we hang out with older senior citizens, we're not reminded of this loss of stature all that much because *all* of us are getting shorter to one degree or another. But I see it and feel it when I'm with sons-in-law, nephews, and their friends. I still don't feel short—for now. Perhaps that will start to happen if my grandchildren turn out to be tall.

For now, I'll just try to appreciate that there are benefits for seniors who are getting shorter. Where really tall folks live, the air is a bit too thin. In certain basements, you could bump your head. When you're way up there, it's harder to see and avoid cracks in the sidewalk. And if they happen to fall, as we are wont to do as we age, they'll have a longer trip to the ground.

29 inches! *Whew!* What a relief!

CHAPTER 25

STRANGE AS IT MAY SEEM, RULES NO LONGER RULE

On the day after my 18th birthday, I was issued a "Registration Certificate" by my local Draft Board. I had dutifully followed the rule that required all males over the age of 18 to register. And while I probably had a month or more to do so, I was the kind of kid who got his weekend homework assignments done on Friday afternoon. So I promptly visited the Draft Board.

Let's face it: this was a rite of passage. It would be another three years before worrying about the massive draft necessitated by the Vietnam War would consume all my waking hours and then some. But back in 1965, getting a draft card seemed, well, cool.

On the back of my draft card was a stern warning that the card should be kept on my "person" at all times. So, it went into my wallet and there it stayed while I finished my undergraduate degree (in the safety of a student deferment); when I took a job in the defense industry in the hopes of getting another deferment (a job I ended up quitting before my Draft Board actually weighed in); when I got reclassified as 1-A when I enrolled in a master's program; and when I eventually failed not one but two draft physicals.

By the time this all played out, I was still only 22, and in theory you could be drafted until you were 35. After my last physical, I was told that I was only ineligible until such time as I had a minor elective surgical procedure. There was always the possibility that someone might abduct, anesthetize, and operate on me, and then rat me out to my draft board.

So in my wallet that draft card stayed.

I mention all this because rules have always played a big role in my life. In an earlier life I studied and actually briefly worked in engineering. Engineering and science were positively brimming with laws (Newton's; Ohm's; Hooke's; et al.) as well as principles (Bernoulli's; Archimedes's) and theorems (good old Pythagoras).

But this proved to be child's play compared to the legal world in which I later came to dwell. There were constitutions, statutes, regulations, and guidances. Federal laws, state laws, local laws and even international laws. There was common law which—it always seemed—judges just made up. There were rules of civil procedure, rules of criminal procedure, rules of appellate procedure, bankruptcy rules, and rules of evidence. And don't forget that bane of all first year law students, the Rule Against Perpetuities (don't ask—it won't be on the test).

And I almost forgot the one we learned in Kindergarten: The Golden Rule.

But speaking of things golden, here's something strange that I've observed in my post-70 golden years: these days, rules are not just made to be broken. Breaking rules has become an end in itself, if not an art form.

You see this on all sorts of TV shows. Take police procedurals. Whenever a couple of cops pull up at a building where the heavily armed perp is known to be holed up, the sergeant back at the precinct house will always tell them to wait for back-up. *Not on your life, Sarge.*

Or take a medical show where a junior surgical resident believes a patient will die without surgery before a licensed attending can get to the hospital. *Scalpel!*

Or perhaps a show about fire and rescue workers who are ordered by radio to get out of a building fully engulfed in flames while a young/old/disabled person remains unaccounted for. *Sorry, Chief, my radio's not working in here.*

Then there are the stories where young, horny and decidedly pre-menopausal folks are reminded to use birth control. *You've gotta be kidding.*

In the spring of 2021, I saw promos on TV for a new show called "Rebel." It was cancelled before I had a chance to sample an episode, but I had a pretty good idea what it was about.

The breaking of rules has also crept into big-time sports—in a big way. In recent years, a major league baseball team came up with a high-tech way of stealing signals. And a professional football team found a low-tech way to lower the air pressure inside a football and shorten its opponents' kicks.

Heck, in 2016 a well-placed minority of American voters elected a president who believed that not a single law, rule or norm should be followed, and he thumbed his nose at all of them. And he came frighteningly close to being reelected in 2020.

I suppose this worship of rule breakers is an extension of our idolization of people who think outside the box. Maybe it all started in the 1960s, when much of our own generation resisted conformity by opting out of daily showers and haircuts.

And what about that rule that you must keep your draft card in your possession at all times? Well, as far as I know, they never rescinded that one. And while no army in its right mind would ever want me (surprise!—I never had that elective surgical procedure!), my draft card still molders in my wallet.

CHAPTER 26

THE STRANGE NEW WAY THAT MEMORIES ARE CAPTURED

As I have discussed elsewhere, I was a camp kid. I attended the same summer camp in the Catskill Mountains every summer from 1955 through 1964, the summer before I started college. Although my camp—like many camps—focused heavily on athletics, and I was a pretty awful athlete, I still loved camp and eagerly awaited the camp season each spring. I formed many friendships during those years, and I remain in touch with a few camp colleagues even today.

One minor ritual took place every summer at my camp and —I suspect—at many other camps. Not many kids had cameras at my camp. And because this was decades before digital photography, taking pictures involved purchasing film, sending it out for development, picking up and paying for the finished prints a week or so later, and hoping that they turned out okay. To remedy the potential loss of camp memories, at my camp, each bunk had to sit for a group portrait.

This was a pretty low-tech affair, even for the 50s and 60s. The two counselors and the eight or so kids in the bunk would assemble outside. The kids would form two rows, with the taller kids behind the shorter ones. The kids were encouraged to wear T-shirts emblazoned with the camp's name; some did, and some didn't. The two counselors would tower over and flank the kids on each side. A placard would be placed in front of the short kids with the name of the camp, the year, and the number of the bunk. Each kid would receive a print, though I imagine we got billed for them.

These camp photos became treasured memorabilia. Every now and then, often in the course of a move when I'd be tossing out old junk, I would come across a camp photo from when I was, say, eleven years old, and get a chuckle. That one print would often represent the only remaining memories from an entire eight-week camp season, so it always avoided the dumpster.

Let us now fast forward some 50+ years to the summer of 2021. My two oldest grandkids went to overnight camp for the first time, having had to forego the experience the previous summer due to the Covid pandemic. Within days, their parents started forwarding to us photos they had received electronically from the camp. In any given week, I would see my grandson playing any and every sport with his usual gusto. In some cases, he was caught with odd expressions on his face, perhaps because he was straining to catch a ball, or cavorting in the water, or getting sprayed with shaving cream. In some, he would be part of a mob of boys where only a small slice of his face was visible.

Are you ready now for one of those "welcome to the 2020s, Grandpa" moments?

After enjoying yet another batch of these photos of my grandson, I asked his parents how the camp managed to pluck out a bunch of pictures of their son, whether it be him alone or part of a group. Surely, they did this for all the kids, right? Was some poor staff member spending his or her summer poring over thousands of photos with a magnifying glass and sorting them into hundreds of buckets?

They just gave me one of those looks. *Seriously, Dad?* And then it hit me:

Facial recognition software!!!!

How could I not have realized that sooner? I watch so many police procedurals where crimes are often solved with the aid of what those in the know call "facial rec." A suspect (i.e., *perp*) is caught on camera (*CCTV*, of course, especially in the U.K.). His face is inputted and lo and behold what emerges is a dude with a criminal record (a *sheet*), not to mention his known associates and his last known address. An arrest follows shortly before the credits roll. While many crimes have been solved with facial rec software, it has been roundly criticized for eroding the right to privacy and the potential for misuse.

So, what we have here is a controversial law enforcement tool—developed to catch murderers and rapists—being repurposed to provide our children with a steady flow of pictures of their own kids getting their money's worth, at a camp where sending one kid for a single season (now seven weeks, down from eight in my day) could have at one time purchased a house free and clear of any mortgage.

I don't know about you. But for me, the word "strange" simply doesn't do it justice.

CHAPTER 27

THE STRANGELY ETERNAL ALLURE OF SIMPLE PLEASURES

My father was a city guy. He lived in apartments all his life. His work required him to travel around New York City, and he knew his way around as well as some cab drivers. An avowed foe of parking spaces that required a payment, he was a master of the alternate side of the street parking rules, and he would often prowl around the penumbra of our neighborhood looking for a space that he wouldn't have to vacate until 11:00 the next morning.

It surprised some people to learn that my urban father liked to fish. From as far back as I can remember, during the warmer seasons, my father routinely spent a Saturday or Sunday fishing in the freshwater reservoirs north of our home in the Bronx. On some occasions, he would go "deep sea" fishing a mile or so offshore on a party boat based in places like Sheepshead Bay in Brooklyn.

He had a pretty complete collections of rods, reels, floats, sinkers, lures, and whatnot for both fresh and salt water. I have trouble recalling where he kept all that stuff in our small apartment. I suppose he kept a lot of it in the trunk of his car—which also enabled him to sneak away for a couple of hours on a slow workday.

By the time my memory kicks in, my father had already corralled my older brother as a reliable fishing buddy. And, in time, I pretty much went along for the ride. Sure, they tried to get me interested in fishing, and I would gamely give it a try on each excursion. That usually ended when, for the third or fourth time that day, I got my line tangled with a nearby tree (making it more likely that I would catch a pinecone than a perch), or when I just plain got bored from catching nothing for hours, whichever came first.

I was a much bigger fan of those occasional deep-sea excursions. I remember them as being feast or famine affairs. On some days, no matter what fish were supposed to be running, and no matter which promising cove the captain would steer the boat into, we came up empty. But on a few occasions, you might catch fish with a vengeance. I can still recall the time I filled up a barrel with wheezing blow fish, reeling them in two at a time as soon as I got my line back in the water.

This was all a very long time ago.

In the past 50 or so years, I maybe went fishing three or four times. I have a son-in-law who is a pretty avid fisherman, and on a few occasions, he would coax me into joining him with one or two of my grandkids. But this was never something I might initiate. And to whatever extent I tried to imagine what retirement might look like for me, it didn't include much fishing.

But a funny thing happened on my 74th birthday. Or, I should say, the day after it.

Weeks earlier, my older brother had asked me what I might like for my birthday. I think I surprised him—and myself—when I asked him to take me deep sea fishing. So in the early afternoon on the day after I turned 74 we boarded a party boat near Atlantic Highlands, New Jersey. He had told me a few days earlier that fluke were running that week. So of course, whenever I shared with one of my kids that we had made these plans, I could not resist adding, "if I catch anything, it will be a fluke."

This is a character flaw that I am unlikely to overcome any time soon.

What I found most remarkable is how little has changed in fishing in the 70 or so years I've been dabbling in it. A fishing rod is still a fishing rod. A reel is still a reel (though I think most folks changed from those old reels that hang below the rods to "spinning" reels that sit atop the rod, sometime around the Eisenhower administration). A hook is still a piece of metal with a loop at one end that attaches to your line and a sharp point on the other end that goes through your bait and then—hopefully—a fish. A sinker is still a dead weight that keeps your hook and bait down where you think the fish are hanging out.

I had a good day! I caught about four fluke, all of which had to be thrown back as too small. But I was struck at how I could still remember that feeling you get when a fish is nibbling on your bait. And it was still a thrill when you pull up, realize you've hooked one, and slowly reel it in.

But of course, a fishing trip isn't just about fishing. I had forgotten how peaceful it can be on a boat a few miles from shore in lower New York harbor, especially with a pandemic surging and surging again on all sides with no end in sight. The only disturbances—other than a catch—came from a nine-year-old boy whose dad had brought him along, and who had run out of patience well before the rest of us. He reminded me of someone I knew many years ago.

Of course, the real reason I had cadged my brother into this fishing trip was this. I couldn't remember the last time my brother and I had just hung out together for a few hours. Just the two of us. No spouses, no chores, no robocalls. Just a chance for two old guys to shmooze and reminisce.

And that, I learned on the day after I turned 74, is a simple pleasure that never gets old.

CHAPTER 28

THE STRANGE MIRACLES OF TWENTY-FIRST CENTURY MEDICINE

In the autumn of 2021, I went out to my mailbox to collect the usual assortment of ads, bills, and whatnot. As I strolled back toward my house, I discovered buried in the pile a piece of certified mail. My first thought: am I in some sort of trouble? When I flipped it over to see who sent it, I was surprised to see it came from the group where my urologist practices. But what could be so important and serious to warrant a certified letter? Had they misread my latest PSA blood test result? Was I suddenly at greater risk of prostate cancer? Or might it have to do with a drug my urologist had recently prescribed for me—maybe some new caution from the FDA?

I'm sure the suspense is killing you, and I promise we will come back to this. You know from the title of this chapter that we are talking here about medical miracles, and I promise you will not be disappointed. But allow me to digress to first discuss two changes in the world of medicine that have come of age—if you will—during our 70s. And these are not one-shot deals like my certified letter, but developments that affect us month after month and even week after week.

First, at the risk of hearing groans from my fellow old-timers, I would like to discuss electronic medical records. As I recall, this was brought to the fore in the months leading up to the passage of the Affordable Care Act early in the Obama administration. Most of us see more than one doctor, and by the time we reach 70, we have more specialists in in our lives than we ever imagined. They all run tests and they sometimes can help us more effectively if they know what other medical data we've accumulated from other doctors, and what drugs they have all prescribed.

Where I live, there is a regional hospital nearby, and most of the doctors in the area are part of a network that shares our medical data on something called MyChart. So for the past few years, whenever I see one of the doctors in this network, I can expect to receive alerts that there are new test results, or visit summaries, or confirmations of my next appointments on MyChart.

Am I the only one who thinks it's revolutionary for patients to have access to raw medical data? It wasn't all that long ago that many believed that patients could not deal with this sort of information unless and until it was interpreted by our doctors. (Think Jack Nicholson in "A Few Good Men": *YOU CAN'T HANDLE THE TRUTH!*) And I will be the first to acknowledge that much of the blood work and other data I see is gibberish to me. But I do know how to spot my cholesterol numbers and compare them with my earlier numbers. And I can usually figure out that a test result that says NORMAL is probably a good thing, and if it says NEGATIVE, that's probably good too.

But this is not the only thing I like about being connected to my doctors electronically, especially at an age where I seem to need more of them and more help from all of them. There is also this: you can type a message to your doctor and get a response!

Did you ever try to phone one of your doctors with a question? Of course, you don't expect them to pick up, when they are most likely to be with a patient. Many doctors will call back within a reasonable amount of time. But some do not. Did you ever watch a TV commercial touting some drug where they try to get you to push your doctor to describe their drug with a line like "Call your doctor to see if drug ABC can help your XYZ condition…." Seriously? Call my doctor?

Perhaps I have been more fortunate than others. But when I send a question to one of my doctors through the messaging "portal," I usually get a response within a day or two, from the doctor or from a nurse passing along the doctor's advice. But let's not tell too many people about this. If the drug companies get wind of this, we will start seeing commercials saying "Send your doctor a message through your portal asking about drug ABC…." Surely the MyChart system would crash.

But I do think it's a bit of a medical miracle to have more information about ourselves and more avenues of improving communications with our providers.

Here's my second medical miracle: Urgent Care! During the Covid pandemic it was a place to get tested and possibly treated, at least initially. But apart from Covid, it has provided a place to get diagnosed and perhaps treated for less than life-threatening illness and injuries. Without an appointment. And they accept Medicare.

In late 2021 I had two occasions to visit the urgent care in my neighborhood. In late August I woke up with a bit of fever and flu-like symptoms. Although I was fully vaccinated and was pretty diligent about wearing a mask, my first fear was Covid. So the first thing they did at urgent care was a rapid Covid test, followed up by the more accurate test; happily, both negative. And here's my favorite part: our local urgent care is connected to the network built around the regional hospital I mentioned. They accessed my records and learned that I had an episode of atrial fibrillation back in 2009 for which I've continued to take a beta blocker. A savvy nurse at urgent care did an EKG and determined I was in A-fib once again. They promptly made me an appointment with my cardiologist for the very next day. (Try doing that yourself some time!)

I was on my way home about an hour after I had arrived.

A few weeks later, I got to visit urgent care again. This time, the diagnosis was stupidity, though they were kind enough not to say that. Early one morning, while making coffee, I had grabbed a knife to try and break off some ice that had built up in my freezer. The knife slipped, and suddenly my left thumb was bleeding with a serious cut. At that visit with my cardiologist, he had put me on a blood thinner. So, I could tell that a Band-Aid wasn't going to do it here. I wrapped up my thumb, threw on some pants, and drove over to urgent care. I hadn't stopped to think about whether it would be open yet. As it happened it was 7:50 AM and they would be opening at 8:00. I was the first patient of the day, and they quickly got me with a nurse who skillfully numbed my thumb, applied a tight row of five sutures, and sent me on my way.

Once again, in and out in less than an hour. Eight or nine days later, without an appointment, I dropped by to get the stitches removed. As I wasn't bleeding and others were ahead of me, I had to wait about ten minutes to be seen. Stitches gone and—I confirmed a few weeks later—no scar.

In an odd way, this reminded me of the days when I was growing up and had to go to "the doctor" in our neighborhood. He was a general practitioner, which I suppose meant that he'd graduated from medical school and hung out a shingle. No appointments; just show up and wait your turn. The receptionist was typically the doctor's wife, who people called a nurse—except that she wasn't. (Yes, wife, not husband. This was before America learned that women could be doctors, from—of all places—the Union of Soviet Socialist Republics.)

And one more thing about the local doc's office: you paid cash. This is why my father pushed me to become a doctor until they day he died.

Of course, at our local urgent care, the nurses are real and highly trained. There may be only one MD on the premises at any given moment, but they have multiple exams rooms and several nurses who can often deal with your problem from start to finish. I can't tell you if they accept cash, but they do accept medical insurance, including Medicare. In my book, figuring out a way to supercharge the old local GP's office counts as another medical miracle of our 70s.

So, now, what about that certified letter from my urologist? I opened it to learn that they were holding about $75 of my money, and they wanted to know what to do with it. I can only guess how this came to pass. I suspect I went for an office visit, gave them my insurance information, and headed home. I probably got billed by the practice and paid it while the insurance claim languished, but then the practice got paid for a second time. The letter suggested that they had contacted me about this, though I don't recall it. But by late 2021, that $75 had become "unclaimed funds," sort of like a bank account that you forget about when you move to a new area and the bank loses track of your address.

The letter asked me if I'd like the urology practice to hold on to the funds and apply them to a future visit, or just send me a check. Take a guess which box I checked. I really and truly like and respect my urologist. But getting that $75 back is right up there with those other medical miracles.

CHAPTER 29

THOSE STRANGE EXTRA DIGITS IN OUR DATES OF BIRTH

At the big box pharmacy I patronize, when I go to pick up a prescription—which I find myself doing more often than I would care to discuss—after I give them my name, they ask for my date of birth. Over time, I have come to realize that they are only interested in the month and the day.

I find that a bit surprising. I am sure you have heard this at one time or another over your long life. If you are at a party and someone wants to bet that two people have the same birthday, if there are 23 people in attendance, the odds are even money. But if there are 75 people at the party, there is a 99.9% chance that two will share a birthday.

I would venture a guess that my pharmacy dispenses a few hundred prescriptions every day. So I cannot help but wonder if my pharmacy is running a risk that some poor soul with the same birthday as I have—who need not be my age— is about to share the unpleasant side effects that many of my drugs seem to exhibit.

But I'm not actually here to bloviate about birth dates getting shortened. Just the opposite. I wish to offer my two cents about them getting *longer*. Allow me to explain.

For most of my life, dates of birth consisted of no more than six digits: two for the month, two for the day, and two for the year. Actually, for us Leos, and others born in the first nine months of the year, we only needed one digit for the month, for a total of just five digits. And for those lucky few born in the first nine days of one of the first nine months, they need just four digits. One of my childhood friends had the cool, compact date of birth of 8/9/47. (Actually, two of them did. See what I mean about that 99.9% probability?)

I cannot pinpoint the date, but perhaps over the last decade or two, four and even five or six digits became insufficient. From that point forward, everyone who wants what we today call our "data" requires a year of birth expressed fully in four digits.

I have spent a good bit of time (OK, maybe an hour or so) pondering why this happened. Maybe it goes back to the end of 1999, during the "Y2K" scare. Remember that? The fear about planes falling out of the sky and the like because the first two digits of the year flipped from 19 to 20, but—even more scary—the last two digits went from 99 to 00. Heavens! How remarkable! But now it's just a memory that sometimes comes back to me when my local deli counter is calling numbers in the high 90s and I'm holding a ticket that says 02.

(Y2K was probably the cause of another pet peeve of mine. For most of my adult life, checkbooks issued by banks included this line for the date: "__________, 19___." I suppose that when Y2K began to loom on the horizon, the banks went bonkers worrying about all those checks that would have to be dumped and replaced when the year no longer began with 19. I foolishly thought they would start printing checks with "___________, 20____." If they did, they wouldn't need to worry about this again for nearly one hundred years. But no! They started sending out checks with just a completely blank line for the date. So now everyone who writes a check will forever have to waste about two seconds writing all four digits of the date. Thanks for nothing.)

I believe there is more to the obsession with eight-digit dates, and here is what I think. The problem is that more and more old codgers are living to ages above 100 years. What does this mean? Well, today, if someone has a date of birth of, say, 10/20/20, they might be a two-year-old in daycare, or someone who is 102 years old ensconced in assisted living.

You would think that the folks mining this data could figure out who this person is without insisting on extra digits in their year of birth. If that person is applying for a credit card, they probably aren't two years old; but if they are, their credit history will likely be a bit too short to issue a card to them. No harm, no foul. If the date of birth is being requested by a tony preschool, the odds are good that the applicant is two years old (though either of them might be in diapers).

So yes, I think we will be using eight-digit dates of birth (yes, get used to that leading zero, fellow Leos) for the duration. Those guys two born on 8/9/47 (August 9, 1947)? Double those digits to *08/09/1947*. All that extra—and largely useless—data taking up space in some cloud or another.

Finally, if anyone is reading this in one of those European countries that places the day before the month, I have nothing to add. If your birth date used to be 8/9/47, meaning (on your side of the pond) September 8, 1947, it too will become 08/09/1947.

And if you happen to pick up one of my prescriptions at my pharmacy? I have no advice to offer, except watch out for those side effects.

CHAPTER 30

THE STRANGE INEVITABILITY OF TURNING INTO OUR PARENTS

The George Washington Bridge is a majestic looking two-level toll bridge spanning the Hudson River, connecting Washington Heights in New York City and the Palisades in Fort Lee, New Jersey. As part of Interstate 95, it carries massive amounts of traffic going to and from New England to the north and the rest of the eastern seaboard to the south.

There are many things I love about the GWB. Here's one: since around 2000, there are hundreds of LED light fixtures that can change color embedded within each of the two towers. The colored lights are usually reserved for major holidays. When driving beneath the span on the Henry Hudson Parkway while the lights are turned on, the view is stunning. And when you are crossing the bridge and travelling under the towers, they knock your (or, at least, my) socks off.

Here's another. In 1976, Woody Allen starred in the movie *The Front.* It is set in 1953, during the McCarthy era, when the House Unamerican Activities Committee was accusing many in the arts of being closet Communists, leading to the artists being blacklisted. Allen's character agrees to be a "front" for a blacklisted television screenwriter in exchange for a piece of the money paid for the scripts. There is a scene that appears to take place in Fort Tryon Park in upper Manhattan, which overlooks the Hudson. In the distant background one can clearly see traffic bustling along on the two levels of the GWB.

But the lower level of the GWB was not opened until 1962. *Oops.*

Finally, here's one more that actually relates to the point of this chapter. When westbound traffic gets over the bridge, it divides off into numerous highways heading in all directions in New Jersey. One of those arteries is the Palisades Interstate Parkway, which more or less hugs the New Jersey shore of the Hudson River up into Rockland and Orange Counties, New York, where it ends at Bear Mountain.

For as long as I can remember, the ramp from the Palisades Parkway to the GWB has had its own toll plaza. Until around 1970, tolls were collected for travel over the GWB in both directions. Since then, tolls are collected only for eastbound crossings into New York, meaning that the payment is for a round trip. Thus, today the toll barrier on the ramp from the Palisades Parkway only collects tolls for cars about to cross the bridge. (When this was initiated, I seem to recall grumbling that people permanently relocating from New Jersey to New York were getting bilked, while those doing the opposite got a free ride. Surprise! Nobody cared.)

On the other hand, cars coming off the bridge toward the Palisades need not stop to pay. However, the skeleton of the portion of the toll barrier that used to collect from New Jersey-bound passengers still remains. (At least this was true in 2022. A plan seems to be afoot to change the entire toll-collecting apparatus—which will probably result in yet another toll hike.)

In any event, when you enter New Jersey off the GWB and head toward the Palisades, if the sun hits at the precisely correct angle during the late afternoon, and if you look up at the skeleton of the toll barrier and squint just a wee bit, you can still make this out:

Cars 50¢

Yes, back in the day, it cost fifty cents to cross the GWB; a dollar for a round trip. Today, for drivers paying cash, the round-trip toll is $16.00.

I have been known to point this out to anyone in the car with me who will listen. Of course, the folks in my car don't have much of a choice. I mention this even if I have pointed this out once before. Maybe more than once. OK, almost certainly more than once.

Where is this coming from? Like most people, while growing up, I had pet peeves about things my parents used to do. Not that I could do much about them. About the only thing I *could* do was to promise myself that I would never do the same things to my spouse, my kids, or anyone else.

The one thing I remember clearly is that I made that promise most emphatically about my parents' propensity to wax fondly about how much cheaper things were when they were young. A hot dog was a nickel. A broadsheet newspaper like the *New York Times* cost a nickel. It drove me crazy. What was the point? Who cares? I vowed never to do it when I got older.

I lied.

I do it all the time. In some instances, it's even about the same items. When I was growing up, a hot dog was fifteen cents! The *Times* was also fifteen cents. And so much more. A candy bar was a nickel, except for Almond Joy and Mounds, which had two separate bars and cost a dime. A gallon of gas was about 33 cents. A James Bond paperback was 50 cents—trust me, I still have several. (Today even the e-book version of this tome will set you back a few bucks, and—you may have noticed—I'm no Ian Fleming.) A trip to see the Yankees play, including round trip subway fare and a seat in the bleachers, was $1.05. A brand-new Volkswagen Beetle was $1,800. Summer camp was $500 for an eight-week season. Tuition, room and board for a year in law school was about $5000. (I recently heard a rumor that some schools now estimate total costs of $90,000. *Per year.*) I think I do this even more often and more annoyingly than my parents did. In fact, I'm sure I do.

This is not the only way this phenomenon manifests itself. Whenever my mouth opens and out comes an especially rancid dose of sarcasm, someone will tell me I'm turning into my father. Someone very close to me recently gifted me a coffee mug filled with M&M's on which was printed, "Sarcasm is My Love Language."

How do we deal with the strange phenomenon of turning into our parents? Sure, we can chalk it up to DNA. They had it and we inherited it. Just as it was inevitable that I would start going gray in my 30s and would need reading glasses when I turned 40, I was destined to obsess about the high cost of living compared with bygone days—and to do so sarcastically. Interestingly, my parents had plenty of good traits, but no one compares me to them on that score.

When I was a mere youth of 60, in *The Postwarriors: Boomers Aging Badly*, I called this "regression toward the gene." I now wonder whether perhaps there's some sort of Gresham's Law of genetics at work here: bad inherited traits drive out good ones.

CHAPTER 31

OLD HABITS DIE HARDER AND GET STRANGER

We are all familiar with weird habits. You know: stuff like eating one pea at a time. Avoiding stepping on lines in the sidewalk while walking. Staring at the ceiling while riding an elevator. We all know people who practice these and other odd habits—sometimes including ourselves.

Thus, it may not surprise you to learn that I am one of those people who need to squeeze every last drop of toothpaste out of the tube. And I take this *much* too seriously.

It begins when I'm about halfway through a tube which, at that point, is all twisty and full of lumps. I will untwist it and flatten it out so that the bottom portion (away from the nozzle) is perfectly flat, and all the remaining toothpaste is bunched up closer to the nozzle. Only then can you really tell if you are getting close to the end game. If

I'm not, I forget about it for a few weeks, and then repeat the process. Eventually, I will get to the point where most—or even all—of the remaining toothpaste is collected in and around the nozzle and the "shoulders" on which it rests.

Here is where many people give up—but not I. I have learned how to apply pressure from under the shoulders and the nozzle to get that last dollop of Colgate to sit on my toothbrush. Only then does brushing my teeth feel like a real accomplishment.

Of course, that is not my only weird habit. There is always my shtick about using a bar of soap in the shower until there is (almost) nothing left of it. It usually takes a few weeks for a cake of soap to start getting noticeably thinner than it started out, and then another week or two to start thinking about the grand finale. In due course, the bar of soap will get very thin—so thin, in fact, that it will often fold in two. When it does, I squeeze the two halves together into a single piece which is smaller in area than the original bar, but maybe twice the thickness before it folded in on itself. But not for long. It, too, will thin out after a few more showers. And then we start closing in on the wrap-up: the wafer-thin slice of soap breaks into pieces that are so small that they can get washed down the drain. Only then will I unwrap a brand-new cake of soap and start the process anew.

I've probably had those two weird habits for decades. But it was only after I turned 70 that weird became *strangely* weird. And it had to do with after-shave balm.

Except for a few weeks around the late 1980s when I grew a mustache and my family laughed me out of the house, I have always been clean shaven. I always use shave cream and a blade, as it gives me the closest shave possible. And I have often liked to apply stuff that smells nice when I finish. Years ago, it was after shave lotion, which smelled good, but often contained alcohol and thus tended to sting when I applied it.

It was not until a cruise I took around the time I turned 70 that I discovered after shave "balms." These are creamy, viscous products that smell nice, but also supposedly moisturize skin, which I guess is a good thing. Along with shampoo, conditioner, and other stuff, the cruise line on which I most often travel equips each cabin with little 1.3-ounce bottles of Bulgari shave balm, which I started to use; and then there was no turning back. It smelled good and felt good. Win-win.

Of course, I knew that one of those little bottles wouldn't last very long once I got home, so I started to quietly accumulate a few extras before leaving the ship. If my current 1.3-ounce bottle was still mostly full, I would hide it so that the housekeepers would think I had run out and would leave another. When I walked the long corridors of the cruise ship and passed the housekeepers' cart, I would look to see if a supply of those little bottles was in reach. (But I usually chickened out of swiping one or two when I saw that I might be caught by a housekeeper or—worse yet—a fellow passenger.)

In due course, in around 2019, my wife lost patience with this silliness and bought me a bottle of Bleu de Chanel after shave balm for Fathers' Day or my birthday. It was a great product. It came in an elegant squarish bottle made of glass that looked opaque but was actually just frosty. When the level inside began to dip down, and you held the bottle up to a light, you could see how much was still there. There was a black cylindrical cap that you pulled off, revealing a little black pump that you pushed two or three times to get your daily smear.

I started to regularly use the Chanel balm after the cruise ship bottles were used up. By the beginning of 2022, when I held the bottle up to the light, I could see that the level had dropped quite a bit. I also learned that the tube which feeds the pump did not drop vertically but arced gently into the lower right-hand corner of the bottle.

This was valuable information, for there came a time when nothing came out when I just pressed on the pump. But what if I stood the bottle on a slight incline, with the left side elevated over the right? The little shave balm that remained would flow down into the lower right-hand corner, where the end of the tube hung out. This yielded another two or three days worth of squirts.

But I wasn't done yet. I was convinced that within the bottle there was still a bit more of the viscous shave balm, but I simply couldn't access it. I then decided that the pump had to come off. I thought it would screw off easily, but it didn't screw off at all. I got a pair of pliers and tried to pop the whole pump mechanism off, but it broke, leaving sharp edges. I knew the game was over, but I still turned the bottle upside down and waited about five minutes to see if a drop or two might still ooze out. None did.

One might fairly ask: where is this coming from? "Waste not, want not"? A real desire to save money? I will sometimes try to calculate how much money I save with these practices. For discussion's sake, suppose I would use a tube of toothpaste for seven weeks without my dumb habit, and maybe I get an eighth week because of it. That would mean about one "free" tube of toothpaste a year. A savings of perhaps $250 in a lifetime? Maybe similar numbers for the bars of soap? Harder to say with the shave balm, as I didn't start shaving 'til well into my teens.

As weird as these habits might be, they should be appreciated as really, truly, strangely weird when viewed in a broader context. Consider how, as we go through life, we are constantly hit with unexpected expenses, large and small, accidental and predictable. Your hot water heater dies. Ka-ching! Your transmission goes. Ka-ching! Your favorite shoes get ruined in a rainstorm. Ka-ching! The list goes on and on. It's always something, except when it's a whole spate of somethings.

Many years ago, a friend of a friend shared with me a useful construct that often helps cushion the blow of these sudden expenses.

He called it "The Get-F*cked Fund." What he does is recognize that, over the course of a year, you are always and inevitably going to have some of these expenses that really suck. So when, say, his dishwasher dies, he just takes money out of the (make-believe) Get F*cked Fund and moves on. No tears, no regrets.

I mention this because it provides a useful counterpoint to my strangely weird habits with regard to toilet articles. In early March of 2022, I had finished off a cake of Dial soap in the shower, and I had gone through my shave balm shenanigans, when I noticed strange symbols on the keypads of our home security system. I called the folks who service it and got this news: my system uses what amounts to a cell phone to call out to the central station when there is a fire, break-in, or whatever. But it wasn't equipped to work in a "5G" area, which mine had apparently become in early 2022. So I needed a new unit which they were happy to install at the discounted price of $536 including tax.

And there it was: a lifetime of saving on soap and toothpaste gone in the blink of an eye.

CHAPTER 32

STRANGE INTERLUDES

If you are over 70, in all likelihood, you have these moments when you can't seem to get out of your own way. I'm reluctant to call them senior moments, because those are just memory lapses, and we've been having those since well before we turned 70. No, this takes things to a new level. These episodes usually involve us (or at least me) making some sort of dumb mistake and doing something inexplicable, pointless or just plain silly. Here are a few of mine that took place during the winter of 2021-2022. If they remind you of your own escapades, bless you: nice to know it's not just me. If not, double check your birth certificate. You probably haven't turned 70 yet.

Right around Christmas of 2021, I was deploying my handy Dustbuster to vacuum the carpet in my car. We had already had one dusting of snow, and I had spread the snow-melting stuff on my front walk in case it were to ice up. It was a reminder that another winter was just beginning, and things were going to get messy on the streets and sidewalks of the suburb where I live.

It was then that it occurred to me that it was time to pull out the carpets from my car and replace them with the rubber mats that protect the car from the salt and slop of winter. But my next thought was this: did I even have rubber mats *for this car*?

Good question, as it turns out.

I had bought this car in July of 2020, when the Covid pandemic was raging through its first wave. Here is how that happened. For a number of years while I was still working full time, my wife and I had owned three cars for the two of us. We had sort of backed into that. My wife and I both commuted to work by car, in opposite directions, and we each needed our own. When our kids got their driver's licenses, they "needed" a car—until they didn't. They couldn't really keep them at college, and when they started to work and live in New York City, they rarely needed them and had nowhere to park, so their cars often sat around in our driveway.

At some point we found ourselves with an extra car and decided to just keep it for a while. Neither of our commutes could be accomplished with public transportation. And neither of us had a co-worker living nearby who could give us an occasional lift. So, we got used to having a back-up car in case there was an unexpected problem with one of our cars and we needed to get to work quickly.

In the final iteration of that three-car situation, two of the cars were viewed as "mine." One was a hybrid sedan with front wheel drive, which was my day-to-day commuting car. I had gotten into the habit (one might call it a fetish) of squeezing at least 100,000 miles out of all my cars; and by mid-2020, this one was well past the 95,000-mile mark. My other car was an older SUV with four-wheel drive and significant mileage. I used it for shlepping stuff, but mostly I drove it in winter driving conditions.

Around the spring of 2020 I had brought the SUV in for routine service, and my bill came with a warning. The fuel pump and other vital organs on this vehicle needed to be replaced and replaced *soon.* Don't ask what this was going to cost. So, I slipped into one of my trademark modes: avoidance. Heck, at that point it wasn't going to snow for at least six months. I'd worry about it some other time. Besides, this was the early pandemic. I wasn't driving to my office or any other destination more than a half hour away, and my hybrid sedan was still doing fine.

But then my granddaughter's birthday appeared on the horizon. She and her family had decamped to eastern Long Island due to the pandemic, and the celebration was going to take place about 100 miles from our home. It dawned on me that we were about to embark on a 200-mile round trip with either a sedan with almost 100,000 miles or an SUV with a fuel pump on its last legs. The thought of our car breaking down far from home while a pandemic was raging was not a happy one.

I decided it was time to trade in my two old cars for one new one. It will not surprise you that buying a new car in the middle of a pandemic proved to be a challenge on many levels. (For example, I had to fetch the title certificates for the two old cars so I could trade them in—but they were stashed in a safe deposit box at my local bank branch, which had closed due to the pandemic.)

I'll be the first to admit that I'm not the most ferocious negotiator when buying cars. But I always did one thing I had learned about many cars earlier: I got the salesman to "throw in" rubber floor mats. (Yes, I know the salesmen get a good laugh in the break room about throwing in a $100 item to avoid knocking $1000 of the sale price. You don't need to rub it in.) This sealed the deal, and we had a brand-new car to travel out to Long Island for the birthday celebration.

This all slowly came back to me 18 months later while I stood in my garage thinking it was time to put on the rubber mats. If I had them—and I felt pretty sure that I did — where exactly were they? Answer: about ten feet away on a shelf in my garage, largely hidden from view by a big cooler chest. As I pulled them out, I had two epiphanies. First, yes, these were the mats designed to fit the new car I had purchased in July of 2020.

The second? They were spotless. No mud, no salt stains, no scuff marks. They looked, felt and smelled brand new. Because they *were* new. Yes, after beating up my car salesman to throw them in back in July of 2020, *I had gone through the entire winter of 2020-21 without even once remembering that I had them.*

But little did I know that this particular strange interlude was not over just yet at Christmastime 2021. On Memorial Day weekend of 2022, I had my first flat tire on the car I bought in the summer of 2020. As I rooted around the cargo area to see what type of spare tire I had, as I lifted the carpet covering that space, I discovered that the salesman had not only thrown in *floor* mats. There in all its glory was a rubber mat under the carpet that covered every inch of the cargo area.

Maybe I negotiated a good deal after all.

It was the afternoon of December 31, 2021—New Year's Eve in the middle of the horrific Omicron surge in Covid cases. I was 74 years old and had three things on my mind simultaneously. As you can imagine, there was no way this would end well.

The first thing was an attempt to return a garment to a department store. My wife had bought it for me several months earlier as a gift, and it had felt a bit snug. I put it aside, hoping that it would feel a bit looser, or I would drop a pound or two; but when I tried it on again on

December 31, it was clear that the garment and I were not meant for each other. Earlier that day I had tried to return it at the store in the mall, but they told me it was too late: no returns after 90 days. However, it dawned on us that my wife had bought the garment online, so maybe we could effectuate the return online.

The second thing on my mind that moment was a rare opportunity to take an afternoon outdoor walk that day. I have already shared with you how I came to be someone who exercises twice a day. This, however, was a golden opportunity: temperatures in the mid-50s in late December, with no rain in the forecast. The only catch: around the time of the winter solstice, in our part of the world, taking a 45-minute walk requires that you start no later than 4:00 PM if you don't want to end up walking in the dark.

The third thing on my mind was ordering our take-out dinner for our FaceTime dinner with old friends. The place we chose was 20 minutes away, and they told us they would be closing around 5:00, this being New Year's Eve.

Here's where it all became too much for my 74-year-old brain to handle.

I first told the restaurant that we didn't want to pick up the food too early, as we weren't going to be eating until around 8:00. So, I first told the restaurant I'd pick it up around 4:00, upon which my wife reminded me that—just 10 or 15 minutes earlier—we had agreed that we'd walk at 4:00.

So I quickly told the restaurant to change our pick-up time to 3:00. As I was placing our order, my wife called out that she was having success in returning that garment online, but I needed to help her with the return form. As we congratulated ourselves for (seemingly) outwitting the department store, I looked at the clock for the first time since all this started.

It was now 3:20 PM, and I was going to be at least 40 minutes late for our 3:00 pick up at the restaurant. And by the time I raced to the restaurant, paid for the food, raced home and put on my sneakers, there was no way we were going to start our walk before 4:15.

Which is what we did. And we lived happily ever after because there was a fourth thing that could have been on my mind that afternoon, but wasn't, until it hit me: by December 31, ten days after the winter solstice, there's about ten extra minutes of daylight.

So there!

For many years now, when I first climb into bed, I read a book or magazine. I rarely last more than five minutes. My eyes close. I drop the book on my chest. I struggle to turn off the light. And I bid another day *adieu*. Nothing remarkable here, right?

One night in the early days of 2022 I started this ritual but quickly discovered that something was amiss. The words on my Kindle seemed blurry. I couldn't figure out why. I first thought maybe my eyes were teary, but they weren't. Next, this being a Kindle, I thought that I had somehow switched to a smaller font and proceeded to enlarge the print. Still blurry.

What was going on here? Had my vision suddenly changed so that I needed new glasses? It seemed inconceivable. I had just had my annual check-up at the eye doctor *three weeks earlier*, and I was assured that my eyeglass prescriptions were unchanged. Was it a sign of something awful like a stroke? What was going on here?

You need a bit of background here. I have been dependent on reading glasses since I turned 40. For a decade or so thereafter, every year or two, I would need more magnification, so I'd get a few new pairs of readers. I had a "downstairs" pair I kept in the kitchen; an "upstairs" pair I kept on my nightstand for reading in bed; and a "pocket" pair I kept in a case in my pocket when I left home.

I always hated tossing out the old ones, though. So I'd keep a couple of old pairs and stash them in odd places of my house, thinking that they were just a wee bit weaker than my new glasses, and I could use them for a couple of minutes in a pinch. One of those odd places was a junk drawer in my bedroom where I kept my wallet, watch, "pocket" glasses, and sundry other stuff.

As I got increasingly anxious about the blurriness, I thought back to earlier in the day. I had used my "downstairs" glasses to read the print edition of the *Times,* as well as bills, junk mail, and so forth, and all seemed fine. Was there a problem with just the "upstairs" glasses I kept on my nightstand?

The nearest other pair of glasses at that moment were my "pocket" glasses which I keep in its case in that junk drawer in my bedroom. I opened the drawer to look for them, and—by happenstance—I noticed what I thought was one of those old pairs that I had replaced along the way. I put them on, looked at my Kindle, and they were *perfect.*

Two questions came to mind. (1) How did my "upstairs" glasses, which are supposed to be on my nightstand, get switched with the old glasses that reside in my junk drawer? (2) Who was responsible?

Let's start with the easy one, question (2). If you think it was anyone but me, you really haven't grasped the strangeness of being in your 70s.

But *how* did it happen? I can only surmise, but here is my working theory. On occasion, I'll be upstairs using my "upstairs" readers and, for some reason, I need to go downstairs. Instead of putting my "upstairs" readers on my nightstand where they belong, I'll take them downstairs with me. So, at this point, two of my pairs of current glasses—the "downstairs" pair and the erroneously relocated "upstairs" pair—will be downstairs at the same time. Then, for some reason, I had to go back upstairs, and it didn't occur to me to bring my "upstairs" glasses back upstairs. That was regrettable, because while I was back upstairs, I needed glasses to read something, and my "upstairs" glasses were not on my nightstand where they should have been.

I then surmise that I went into my junk drawer. Perhaps I was thinking my "pocket" glasses were there. Maybe they were, and I didn't see them, or maybe they were elsewhere. What does seem probable is that I saw a loose pair of glasses in the drawer, used them (or discovered that they weren't very good anymore), and I put those old glasses down on my nightstand. And when I used those old glasses that night, I thought I might be having a stroke.

If I'm being honest, I have no real idea if any of this stuff actually happened. What I do know is that an old pair of glasses found its way onto my nightstand and was impersonating my current readers.

And therein lies the terribly strange thing about being in your 70s. Not only do you do strange stuff. Even worse, sometimes you can't even reconstruct how or why you did it.

On a cold afternoon in January 2022, I walked out my front door to go to the mailbox at the curb. As I was returning to my house, I noticed that two garage doors were open, the one I use with my car and the one my wife uses with hers. Like many in suburbia, we have automatic garage door openers that can be operated from our cars when we return home. Each unit also has a button near the door that leads from the garage into our house which opens or closes the unit. And we also have a panel outside the garage doors that can open one door by entering a code. Perhaps the most salient fact for this discussion is that we almost always keep both garage doors closed, and we keep the door from the garage to the house locked.

Fresh from my inconclusive resolution of the switched eyeglass caper, I went into high gear. This time I came up with a theory that actually seems to make sense. The day before I found the two open doors, I had gone out the front door of my house to get the mail, and I found that our trash had been picked up. So, after fetching the mail, I grabbed the empty trash can and headed toward the garage, where we keep the trash cans. As no door was open, I used the panel and the door opened to the bay where my wife's car lives. After dropping off the empty trash can, I headed toward the door into the house.

Here is where you need to watch me carefully, perhaps in slow motion.

With the mail in my right hand, I use my left to put the key in the lock and open the door. (Remember, I had walked out the *front* door, so the door from the garage was locked.) I then push the button to the left of the door to close the garage door in my wife's bay and walk into the house. I'll bet you guessed it: instead of pushing the button to *close* the door in my wife's bay—and, of course, without paying attention—I pushed the other button which *opened* the garage door in my bay. So instead of ending up with two closed doors, I had two open doors.

I sometimes think my life is becoming a somewhat tired syndicated police procedural in which I play the perpetrator, the victim *and* the detective.

In late January of 2022, I awoke to find a text on my cell phone. It appeared to come from our bank, and it said that they suspected fraud as to a substantial check they had cleared. It urged me to take one action if the check was legitimate and another if it was not.

Aha! Defenses up! I read the AARP magazine with all those articles about seniors being scammed. This was a trick! *How ingenious*, I thought: *pretending to be policing and protecting me from fraud while committing fraud!*

Well, I was not about to call the number recited in that text. But I did feel a wee bit of concern that maybe it was legitimate. So I found a number that I knew belong to my bank, and called. After the usual menus and whatnot, I learned that the text was legit, and the fraud had indeed been perpetrated.

In due course, I was able to view the phony cleared check online. These crooks were not subtle. They had printed a check with our info and account number, but in a form that was very different from the checks we had been using for many years. They made it payable to someone I never heard of and entered a signature that bore no similarity to mine.

The whole episode was disconcerting. It appeared that someone had gotten hold of one of our real checks, and they were off to the races. How could we prevent this from happening again? We actually don't write all that many checks, preferring to rely on online bill payments. But all it took was for one thief to get one quick look at one check, and they were in business.

I was impressed that my bank picked up that this one check was a fraud, but a little less impressed that they did so *after* they had cleared it. But my bank promptly restored the funds and helped me to quickly set up a new account with a new number. Of course, it was more complicated than that. A lot more complicated. We had a number of direct deposits and debits linked to our old account, and they all had to be changed. We pay several recurring bills online, so that had to get switched over from the old account to the new one. And I use an ATM regularly to withdraw cash and deposit checks, and that too needed to change. But in due course, it all seemed to be falling into place.

At that point I had a check I needed to deposit and was running a bit low on cash. So I ventured out to the local branch office of my bank, planning to deposit the check and get some cash at the ATM. The particular bank branch I frequent has drive-through ATMs located in the bank's parking lot across the street. So I rolled up, inserted my card—and it didn't go in. I was pretty sure the problem wasn't with my card; something seemed to be blocking the slot. I parked my car and went across into the branch, passing through a lobby, and spoke with one of the tellers.

Here's where you need to watch me closely once again.

The teller assured me I could make the deposit and withdraw the cash with her assistance, and both transactions would use my new account. We processed the deposit and they gave me a receipt. Then we processed the cash withdrawal and she gave me the cash and a second receipt. (Yes, if you think it's odd for a bank to give you a "receipt" for a transaction where the bank doesn't receive anything, you're not alone.)

As I started to leave the bank office, the teller casually mentioned that in the future, if the drive-through ATM is not working, I can always use the one in the "lobby." Really? I had never noticed one. As I exited the branch though what I thought was the lobby, I looked for an ATM, but didn't see one. I went back inside and learned that the "lobby" ATM is actually back across the street in a little building attached to the drive-through lanes. In the 15 plus years I had used this drive-through ATM, I had never even noticed the little building, let alone another ATM inside.

I walked in, determined to try a real ATM transaction using my old card and my new account. It worked! I was elated. I got into my car and headed home. I hit a bit of traffic and as I waited for a red light to change, I reminded myself that when I got home, I needed to record three transactions in my checkbook. I absentmindedly fingered the receipts in my coat pocket and pulled them out to look at them. There was the receipt for the check deposit and the cash withdrawal from the teller inside. But where was the receipt for the ATM transaction in the "lobby" of the little building?

And then it hit me. I quickly turned around, slogged through the same traffic, parked again next to the drive-through lanes, and rushed into the "lobby" of the little building. And there it was: in that little room, which was littered with crumpled receipts, there was mine, dangling out of the slot. Waiting for the next thief to grab it and rip me off again. Me—security conscious me!

(When I said to watch me carefully, I'll bet you thought I left without my cash. Shockingly, I did not.)

Of course, that receipt didn't have my full account number. But it did have a few digits, and who knows what mischief that could have led to.

Several chapters ago, I made the point that sometimes you really can teach an old dog new tricks. You can. But let's face it: some of us old dogs will forget some of those new tricks in about ten minutes.

For the past few years, I have taught a class at a nearby law school. It doesn't pay much and it takes up a lot of time, but I do enjoy it. I was asked to teach the course in the Spring of 2022, and so I got prepared back in the Fall of 2021.

Having taught the course before, I had the basic plan for the course pretty well laid out. The law school requires that I prepare a "syllabus" which includes the reading assignments for each of my Thursday evening class sessions. I keep a three-ring binder with 14 tabs, one for each class, which includes the reading materials for that class and my own class outline. Each time I teach the course, I try to fine tune it with newer or more interesting materials.

On March 7, I decided to prepare for my March 10 class, the ninth of the semester. I went to my binder, opened to tab 9, pulled out the materials for what I will call Topic A, and reviewed them.

A day or two later, but before the class, I got to thinking about Topic A and Topic B, which would be covered a week later on March 17. It struck me that it was more logical to cover Topic B *before* Topic A, not after. I pulled out my syllabus and—sure enough—three or four month earlier, I had swapped out Topics A and B in the syllabus, so that Topic B was scheduled to be covered on March 10. But I hadn't swapped the two sets of materials *in my three-ring binder.* So I quickly prepared to cover Topic B on March 10, trying to imagine the scene if I hadn't had that epiphany: *a classroom in which the only person who wasn't prepared for the class was the instructor.*

But here's the good news: I was already prepared for the class the following week, on March 14.

Unfortunately, we're not quite done here.

On March 10, I arrived at my classroom about 15 minutes before class was scheduled to begin. A group of my students were chatting about my class and other course obligations. I overhead bits and pieces of their conversation: "I was going to do that during the break….this paper is due right after the break…I won't have much time to chill during the break…."

Wait. What?

What break? Spring break? When?

Next week?

I pulled out my trusty syllabus and, sure enough, the tenth class of the course, which would cover Topic A, was scheduled for two weeks later, on March 24. There was no class on March 17 due the Spring break.

And so I now had to conjure up a scenario even stranger than being the only one in the room who wasn't prepared for the class. But for my fortuitous overhearing of chatter among my students….

I pictured myself showing up on March 17 as the only person in the classroom, the only one in the building, and the only one on campus.

CHAPTER 33

HARD-WIRING IS A STRANGELY PERMANENT CONNECTION

I listened to a lot of radio when I was young. Most of the time it was listening to pop songs, both new ones and the hits from years past. Yes, I listened to Yankee games on radio, especially when they played a mid-week away game that wasn't televised. I didn't get my driver's license until I passed my driving test on the third try, when I was around 20, so I didn't do much listening in a car. I did play the radio in our apartment, and everyone in those days had a small, portable, battery-operated "transistor" radio that you could take to the beach.

When rock music got a bit too jarring for my taste in the late 1960s, I started to gravitate toward "oldies" stations. Not too many rock songs were more than five or ten years old, but I enjoyed them more than some of the newer stuff. When I went to college in the late 1960s in upstate New York, there was a really good rock station, WTRY (Great

98!), which played a lot of oldies. When I started to go to reunions every five or ten years after graduation, whenever I got in listening range of WTRY, I would tune in and they seemed to be playing the same songs as they were on all my prior trips north—which I loved.

Around the beginning of this century, satellite radio made an appearance, and I was an early subscriber. For many years, I had a long car commute, so satellite really came in handy. They really had their "oldies" act together. Channel 4 was oldies from the 1940s; Channel 5 from the 1950s; and so forth.

The music on Channel 4 wasn't really for me—mostly "big bands" which I enjoyed every now and them, but which probably appealed more to people a decade or so older. Channel 5 did not have that much rock music that I really enjoyed. So I mostly bounced back and forth between Channels 6 and 7—for as much as two hours a day, every work day. When the pandemic of 2020 and my forced retirement ended my daily commute, I allowed my subscription to satellite radio to lapse. (And around that time Channel 4 stopped playing music from the 1940s. I guess there were no longer enough octogenarians whose car keys had not been confiscated to make it worth Sirius-XM's while.)

At some point I cannot pinpoint right now, I figured out how to download songs to my phone. And at some later date I learned how to play them in my car. So if none of my favorite songs happened to pop up on satellite radio or (I love this term) terrestrial radio, I could listen to them from my phone.

I sometimes wonder how many times I have heard certain songs over the last sixty or so years. *It's Over* by Roy Orbison (1964)? *Tuesday Afternoon* by the Moody Blues (1967)? *The Age of Aquarius* by the 5th Dimension (1969)? *Your Song* by Elton John (1970)? *Piano Man* by Billy Joel (1973)? Hundreds? Easily. Thousands? Could be.

If you are around my age, there is a good chance you remember a TV show in the 1950s known as *Name That Tune*. A song would start to play, and the contestants would try to recognize the song from as few bars as possible. Watching at home, I got pretty good at it. In later years, listening to the radio in my car, an oldie would start playing and I would immediately yell out the name of the song and the artist to the empty seats in my vehicle.

It wasn't that I had any special talent. Few people know less about music than I do. It's just that after a certain number of repetitions, those old songs got *hard-wired into my brain.*

And then there was *West Side Story*. This was the 1962 movie version, following the 1957 Broadway musical.

I became obsessed with it. I bought the album (we're talking vinyl here) and played it incessantly. I loved so many songs: *Something's Coming; Maria; Somewhere; Cool.* My favorite bears the unhelpful moniker *Quintet*, but it is really the prelude to the rumble, in which—all at once—the Jets and the Sharks predict victory and blame the other gang for starting the hostility, while Tony, Maria and Anita have romance on their minds. I not only knew every line of every song. I knew the instrumental riffs that preceded the singing, how many seconds elapsed between the songs, and even where the scratches had been inflicted by my asking too much of a piece of vinyl.

When I went to camp the summer of 1962, I was a waiter. The whole bunch of us shared the *West Side Story* obsession. One day, the dozen or so of us marched out of the kitchen into the dining area in single file, strutting like 15 year old thugs. We were wearing white T-shirts on which we had written the name of a member of the Jets. The alpha dog of our group was Riff. The handsomest of the bunch was Tony. I, one of the least cool of the group, was Ice—the Jet who sang *Cool* after the deadly rumble in the 1962 version. We were holding empty metal trays up high with one hand and snapping our fingers on the other, while we sang "When you're a Jet you're a Jet all the way...."

Almost six decades later, in 2021, Steven Spielberg directed and co-produced a remake of *West Side Story*, and I had to see it. I was stunned at how wonderful it was. There were of course changes, including the creation of a new character for Rita Moreno, who had crushed the role of Anita in 1962. The photography was beautiful. The mostly young cast had great voices, and all the songs from 1962 were still there, though a bit shuffled in sequence.

But what hit me like a ton of bricks were the instrumental riffs within and between songs. They seemed *identical* to those in the 1962 version. I have no idea if they simply copied and pasted portions of the audio from 1962 or meticulously recreated them. But I knew with certainty that they were *identical* because those pieces had been hard-wired in me for more than half a century.

It is strange—even terribly strange—that within the brains of senior citizens there are vast regions that erode a bit every day as we forget more and more things. But there seems to be another zone where things are not just hard-wired but encased in concrete and buried in a vault of the type we see in bank heist movies.

Which brings to mind a line from *West Side Story* that didn't seem all that significant back in 1962. It is the final cut, after Tony, Bernardo and Riff have all been killed. It now seems to have taken on a strangely special meaning for those of us over 70:

There's a place for us….

CHAPTER 34

STRANGELY ENOUGH, IT TURNS OUT THAT BOREDOM IS PREVENTABLE AND CURABLE

In almost every discussion about retirement, the subject of boredom comes up. If you stop working full time—and especially if you retire completely—will you be bored? If so, what will you do? No matter how inherently energetic one tends to be, having extra time on your hands requires some adjustments.

Long before turning 70, I was generally acknowledged to be a pretty boring guy. If you've gotten this far in this book, you know that already. So, when forced retirement coincided with a pandemic, people around me expressed concern. They would ask me how I'm doing with some regularity.

Turns out: pretty well.

For starters, with the benefit of hindsight, I can see that some personal quirks I have had for quite some time have been efforts to make my life just a wee bit unpredictable and just a drop less boring. For example, when I drive somewhere for a social engagement or whatever, I will always find a route home that differs from the route I took to get there, even if it takes longer. (Remember, this is a guy that obsesses about maps and geography. I actually *enjoy* getting lost!)

And then I have cultivated some rather silly attempts to mix things up. For example, I am a big fan of cold cereal and milk as my typical day-to-day breakfast. I have a clear favorite: Quaker Simply Granola. But I will not and do not eat it every day. Too boring. Instead, I rotate it with Kashi Crunch, Raisin Bran Crunch and Cinnamon Life. They're all good, but not quite as good as my granola. I may get a bit disappointed if it's a Life day, but at least granola is never more than three days away, and is always something to look forward to.

Speaking of food, consider this attempt to create excitement and minimize boredom. In early 2022, in an effort to roll back my calorie consumption just a tad, I went on a kick to eat berries and cottage cheese for lunch on Mondays through Thursday. Sound boring? Of course, it does. It *is* boring. But it doesn't have to be. I like both strawberries and blueberries. And my preferred brand of cottage cheese comes in a few varieties, my favorites being Whipped and Everyday. So here is my menu: Monday, strawberries with Everyday; Tuesday, blueberries with Everyday; Wednesday, strawberries with Whipped; and Thursday, blueberries with Whipped. Four days, four different lunches!

I never said this was normal behavior.

Then there's deodorant. The brand I use—Speed Stick—comes in a variety of fragrances. For many years now, I have alternated between two different fragrances. That is, I did so until right around my 74th birthday in August of 2021. We were out of town on a brief trip and when I went into my toiletry kit, I could not find the deodorant, so I popped out to the local CVS and bought one. Later in the trip I made one of those discoveries that I make all too often these days: I hadn't looked hard enough in my kit, where there was most certainly a deodorant. When I got home, I wasn't sure what to do with the new one, so I just placed it into my daily rotation, in which I now happily toggle every day between *three* different fragrances.

In an August 2020 issue of *The New Yorker,* Margaret Talbot surveyed the considerable literature about boredom and took away this insight from a discussion with one social psychologist. She suggested that activities may or may not be engaging and/or meaningful. Thus, reading the same book to a toddler for the umpteenth time is not engaging but might be meaningful. On the other hand, a jigsaw puzzle or the seventh episode of a Netflix series may be engaging but not meaningful. The big prize is an activity that is both engaging *and* meaningful. If neither, Talbot describes it as "a one-way ticket to dullsville."

I believe Ms. Talbot is on to something. I've already shared with you how deeply I've gotten into puzzles. And I've watched more Netflix series than I can count. So I haven't really suffered from a lack of engaging (if not meaningful) activities.

What about my part-time work? I have had few occasions in my career to work on matters that were really meaningful, though they were all challenging to some degree, and that kept me going for decades. Now? Still engaging, though even less meaningful than when I was really in the game.

To my surprise, my part-time, sometime teaching gig has scored high on both scales. Having taught the same course three times, it's not quite as engaging as when I started teaching the course, though I do like to tweak it at times. But I do feel I'm doing something useful for my students in trying to get their arms around a somewhat complicated and challenging field.

But nothing in my life is as engaging *and* meaningful as time spent with my grandchildren. I never tire of hearing what's on their minds. And I often find myself wondering if I am playing a role in creating memories that will stick with them after I am gone.

So, if I am on my way to dullsville, I'm not quite there yet. And by the time you read this, I will be half-way through my 70s.

Am I bored? Not at all.

And, in case you were wondering, I have no plans to take up golf.

CHAPTER 35

OLD FRIENDS: THE POLAR OPPOSITE OF STRANGERS

We began this exercise with me obsessing about Paul Simon and Art Garfunkel—then in their late 20s—telling us in a song called *Bookends* how terribly strange (it appeared to them) to be seventy years old. But we haven't really discussed the lyrics of that song which preceded that line, which discuss how old friends were sitting on a park bench. They characterized the two elderly friends as "bookends." So before we call it a day—or a decade—let us consider for a bit what constitutes "old" friends when we are in our 70s, and the likelihood of our sitting with them on a park bench.

I have had the great fortune in life to make friends during almost every stage of my existence. I met my oldest friend, who I will call D, in third grade—1955. We were what today would be called "besties" through high school. While I am not sure how much time we spent sitting on benches, we did spend time in parks. There were two city parks across from the block on which I grew up, and a huge complex of baseball diamonds a few blocks from D's home. What I remember best, though, is a trip which D and I took to Central Park in Manhattan around junior high school. I don't know if it had anything to do with school, but we were interested in rocks, and—armed with hammer and screwdriver—we went "prospecting" in the heart of New York City. After high school, D and I stayed in touch, sometimes sporadically, through the ensuing decades. We have not sat on a park bench together lately, but we talk on the phone, email, and have dinner together every now and then. When we do talk, we still finish each other's sentences.

Another valued old friend I will call M. We grew up in distant parts of the Bronx. We met in around 1961 through my cousin, who lived near M, and then we went to the same high school where we became friends. From there we ended up at the same college, where we roomed together for two years and pledged the same fraternity. After that, we weren't in touch very often, but at least we saw each other every five years for our college reunions. I cannot recall any park benches we shared, though we did share a pair of seats at Yankee Stadium just a bit before we turned 70.

At the beginning of college, in 1964, I met a friend I'll call K. He was also a fraternity brother, but early in our junior year, he decided to transfer to another college. We lost touch on and off for a while, but for the last decade or two we have spent a lot of time together, even though we live about two hours apart. For several years we have spent New Year's Eve together, including Zoom dinners during the Covid pandemic, even though I can barely stay awake past 11:00 PM.

In 1971 I met S when we entered graduate school together. We have never really lost touch. S is a world—and worldly—traveler, and some of my best memories are of a trip to an exotic locale that S and his family organized to celebrate S's 50th birthday with a posse of friends and their kids. S always was—and remains—a truly remarkable person. And a devoted friend.

So, I have known each of these friends for at least half a century. By any reasonable definition, they are old friends, not just because we've known each other for so long, but because each of us is just plain *old.* And I worry about them. Not all of them are in good health as I write this. And I have already shared the fact that I lost a couple of close friends back in my 50s.

As far as park benches go, I don't know if that will happen any time soon. Yes, we will talk and email and get together when we can. But our circumstances and domiciles usually don't have our paths crossing in a park, especially in the northeast, in good weather. Still, if the stars align and if they are game, so am I.

If you will forgive this from a guy who never had a liberal education, perhaps the park bench scene is a bit of a metaphor. To me, it isn't really about physical proximity. It's more about decades of shared experiences among a couple of old folks who could write each other's obituary, or maybe even a whole biography.

Paul Simon and Art Garfunkel themselves are now over 80. I have no idea if they consider themselves old friends, though what I read about their rifts suggests they are not. And how could they, really? Their identities were so closely tied to each other for decades. Perhaps the recipe for old friendship needs one more ingredient that those two old men sitting on that park bench did not have, at least at that moment.

Space.

CHAPTER 36

THE TERRIBLY INEVITABLE FINAL VERDICT

So how did they do? Simon & Garfunkel, that is. Did they get it right when they sang, "How terribly strange to be 70"? Let us try to unpack that seemingly simple question.

First of all, is it *strange* at all to be in one's 70s? I personally think this a no-brainer. *Of course,* it is strange. We have explored dozens of ways in which the ostensibly linear process of aging seems to take a somewhat non-linear jump into uncharted territory when we begin our eighth decade. We are no longer middle-aged, and it gets harder and harder to remember being young. Of course, it may not happen abruptly on our 70th birthday. But sooner or later, as the years keep going by, there is this growing feeling that life is, well, different. And different in many ways, some good, some not so good.

I am also going to stick my neck out and express my view that, on the whole, for most of us, being in one's 70s is not *strangely terrible.* Yes, some of our contemporaries have suffered and will suffer terribly from illness, loss of a loved one, financial distress, or some other terrible misfortune. For some, their tragedy will color everything else in their lives. For others, though, there may be wonderful things that balance out the terrible: remission or cure; new grandchildren; an unexpected inheritance; a new relationship; etc.

Yes, I opined earlier that the Covid pandemic of 2020-2022 (if 2022 is when it ends) was strangely terrible. But even with the pandemic, there can and likely will be various forms of recovery. Vaccines helped rescue us in 2021, and new drugs to treat Covid have lessened its severity. The economy is likely to go through various gyrations as a result of the pandemic, but may someday return to normalcy—whatever that really is. Other effects will likely be lasting. For better or for worse, the emergence and maturation of video conferencing is a major development, as is the growing (though far from unanimous) recognition that not all people need to toil in a central workplace.

When we focused on the pandemic earlier, we considered other events that might provide a precedent. The terrorist attacks of September 11, 2001? The people we lost then are still remembered. But the buildings that fell have been replaced by a beautiful new tower. The war in Afghanistan that the attack precipitated has itself ended (albeit after 20 years, and not in any satisfying way).

The Cold War, including the Cuban Missile Crisis and Vietnam? It ended around 1990. But some believe Russia's unprovoked attack on Ukraine started a new Cold War. The more things change....

There is one thing about aging that is qualitatively different. We are *never* going back to being middle aged. We may make a fresh start with a new career or business, or a new significant other, or a new home. But we are still old and some of us are still getting older. And that's the terribly good news.

So, at the end of the day, is it terribly strange to be 70? I surely can't answer that question for anyone other than myself. For me, every new decade of life has been an excursion into strange territory. I'm inclined to say that 70 is a bit like 60 on steroids. It is terribly strange. But it is not strangely terrible.

Of course, any birthday with a zero, like 40 or 50, is a milestone and represents aging. Some like to say that any age is "just a number." For all the reasons I have collected here, in my humble opinion, 70 is more than "just a number." It is a very large number. And it is more than that number.

To those of you who are now in their 70s, stay well and stay safe, fellow boomers. Let's touch base if we are still around when 80 arrives.

Now that is going to *really* be strange.

CPSIA information can be obtained
at www.ICGtesting.com
Printed in the USA
JSHW020340180622
27222JS00001B/21